WALL STREET
STOCK SELECTOR

A REVIEW OF THE STOCK MARKET
WITH RULES AND METHODS
FOR SELECTING STOCKS

WILLIAM D. GANN

FOREWORD

The aim and object of every trader who enters Wall Street is to make money, yet it is a well-known fact that a large percentage of traders lose money. There are many reasons for their losses. One of the most important is that they do not know how to select the right stocks to buy and sell at the right time. I expect to give rules provable and practical which will help traders to study and learn how to select the proper stocks to buy and sell with a minimum of risk.

The main object of this book is to bring TRUTH OF THE STOCK TAPE up to date and give the investor and trader the benefit of seven more years of my experience, which has been valuable to me, and if the reader will profit by my experience, it will prove valuable to him.

In this life we must have some definite aim or hope to attain happiness. Money will not bring all of it. Neither can we always help others with money. The best way that I know of to help others is to show them how to help themselves. Therefore, knowledge and understanding properly imparted to others is the greatest good that we can do for them and at the same time do good for ourselves. Thousands of people have written me that I have helped them through TRUTH OF THE STOCK TAPE. I believe the WALL STREET STOCK SELECTOR will give you more knowledge, will bring you more happiness through money gained, than any other book. If it does, I will be well repaid for my labor.

- W. D. GANN

CONTENTS

CHAPTER VI

CHAPTER VII

CHAPTER VIII

CHAPTER IX

CHAPTER I
NEW ERA IN STOCKS OR CHANGED CYCLES

During 1927, 1928, and the first half of 1929, there was much talk of a new era in the stock market and the great value of the Federal Reserve Bank in preventing panics. Many economists, bankers, large financial operators, and businessmen said that the day had passed when there would be panics caused by money conditions such as had happened in 1907 and previous years. At the same time these people were talking about the millennium in financial affairs and the stock market, but they seemed to have forgotten what happened in 1920 and 1921. The decline of 1920 and 1921 following the great bull campaign of 1919 was due to "frozen loans" and tight money. The Federal Reserve Bank was in existence at that time, but that did not prevent Liberty Bonds from declining to around 85 and stocks from selling to the lowest levels on averages since 1914 before the World War began. I quote an article which appeared on November 28, 1927, in one of our leading newspapers. This article was headed "Goodbye, Business Cycle."

"The bugaboo of a 'business cycle' has lost much of its terror-inspiring influence. Scientific management seems to have overcome it. Years ago much was heard of recurring periods of prosperity and depression, and so-called prophets of business, mostly self-styled, were wont to discourse on business cycles, to the great alarm of industry and finance. These prophets proclaimed that business moved like the waves of the ocean and that the higher the waves the deeper the gulf between them They said that the was true of business, and for a long time they had the country scared to their own considerable profit from their necromancy.

"But the spell has been broken and the pall of their prophecies has been dispelled. Businessmen in all lines are freed of the fetish. They realize that 'the business cycle' was a scarecrow. They know that there is no occasion for such a thing if business is held to an even keel. All that is necessary to so hold the rudder is common sense, co-operation and good judgment. There remain a few 'cycle' croakers, but their throats are hoarse from ineffective incantations, and business is going on in a highly prosperous way with no 'cycle' upheavals in lo, these many years, and with no threat of one. Business has seen greater boom times but never was on a more substantial basis, because businessmen have learned how."

It is easy to see how confident this writer was, how he winds up his article by saying, "Business has seen greater boom times but never was on a more substantial basis because businessmen have learned how." This writer was honest and conscientious; of that I have no doubt, but he was either ill-informed or incompetent. He had not gone far enough back in the past to know that history repeats in the stock market and in business.

Late in the fall of 1929 the worst stock market panic in history occurred and was followed by a slump in business, thus proving the theory that cycles do repeat, and while we may have been in a seeming new era, we were only repeating an old cycle or condition which always follows years after wars.

9

HOW TRADERS WERE FOOLED ON CYCLES

Many of the old-time veterans of Wall Street made just as bad mistakes in the 1921 to 1929 Bull Campaign as the rankest lamb.

Many people who had never studied the records of stock markets further back than 1901 to 1921 - and some of them never reviewed them that far back - had the idea, from what other people wrote or said, that a bull market never lasted more than two years. This was the wrong idea which cost many traders heavy losses. After stocks advanced from 1921 to 1923, declined in 1924 and started up again after Mr. Coolidge was elected, and advanced in 1925, traders considered that according to the old rule the bull campaign was over and went short, with the result that they took heavy losses. They continued to fight the market at different times during the bull campaign, thinking that every time the market advanced to a new high level, it would be final top. Certain stocks continued to advance into 1929. Many of these veteran traders made the final mistake, which was worse than any of the first mistakes, of getting bullish at the end of the 1929 Bull Campaign and buying stocks, with the result that they suffered heavy losses in the panic which followed.

There are now over 1500 stocks listed on the New York Stock Exchange against about half this number in 1924. New groups have developed; new leaders have come to the front; new millionaires have been made under new conditions and old millionaires have been unmade. The old-time leaders of the stock market, who failed to change with conditions and applied the old rules, have gone broke. It is reported that Livermore measured the average swing of stocks in 1924 and 1925 and found them too high, according to rules he had previously used; then he went short of the market, lost a fortune, retreated, tried the market again in 1927 and again failed to properly gauge the right time to sell stocks and finally retreated and attacked in 1929, and made a fortune in the panic.

PANICS FROM 1814 TO 1929

Before going into details of the cause of this greatest Wall Street panic, it is important to review the other panics in the United States and in Wall Street over a long period of years and what caused these different panics.

Many factors contribute to the cause of panics. The principal and most important cause of all panics is high money rates, which are due to overextended credit and over speculation. Some of the other causes are undigested securities, both stocks and bonds, or low prices of commodities and foreign exchange, over trading both in business and the stock market, bank failures, exports and imports, price of silver, copper, iron and other basic commodities. If prosperity runs for a long time and stock market prices continue to advance over a period of years, the public becomes overconfident; moves in the markets and business reach the gambling stage. Everybody becomes optimistic and gets the gambling fever and continues to buy until everything is overdone and prices reach a level not warranted by business conditions or the earnings of the corporations of the various industries. When this stage is reached, money gets scarce; banks get loaded up with loans on stocks after a great rise and liquidation has to follow.

The panic of 1814 was due to poor export business and overextended loans. The 1818 panic was again due to money conditions. The banks were overextended. The panics of 1825 and 1826 were due to high money, high discount rate in England, and a decline in commodities, especially cotton. The 1831 panic was caused by high money rates, too rapid expansion in loans and overextended business operations. The panic in 1837 to 1839 was caused by over speculation and tight money conditions. Banks had to cease making specie payments. In 1839 the largest number of banks failed of any time up to that time. The 1848 panic was due to an increase in the number of banks and paper money in circulation and to low price of commodities, especially wheat, corn, and cotton, which this country at that time was largely dependent upon for prosperity. The 1857 panic was one of the worst in history up to that time. This was again due to too much paper money in circulation. For every dollar in gold and silver, there was about $8 worth of paper money circulating. There were a large number of bank failures and banks had to suspend payments. The 1861 panic was due to the Civil War. The 1864 panic was due to war, business depression and tight money. Stocks had also had a big advance, which had tied up a large amount of money in loans. In 1869 the panic was mostly a Wall Street panic. The "Black Friday" occurred in September 1869. This was due to a long wave of speculation, which followed the Civil War and stocks had advanced to extreme high prices. The money rate at that time was the highest of any time since 1857 and 1860. The 1873 panic was one of the worst panics after the Civil War and was due to a large extent to conditions brought about by the war. However, over speculation was one of the prime causes for this, also high money rates at that time advanced to the highest level since 1857.

On September 18, 1873, the failure of J. Cook, National Trust Company, Union Trust Company and other banks brought about serious financial conditions. On September 20, 1873, the New York Stock Exchange closed for the first time in its history and remained closed for 10 days until September 30. The rate of discount at this time was 9 per cent and banks suspended payments. The 1884 panic was due to over speculation in stocks; gold flowed out to Europe and reserves were very low. There were big failures at this time, among them the failure of Grant & Ward. Call money had been high for several years preceding this panic, reaching a high of 30 per cent in 1882, 25 per cent in 1883, and 18 per cent in 1884. The panic of 1890 was largely influenced by over speculation and high money rates. In 1889 call money reached a high of 30 per cent and in 1890 was up as high as 45 per cent. Commodities had reached the lowest levels since the Civil War, which helped to bring about business depression. The failure of Baring Brothers in London precipitated this panic. The 1893 panic was again brought about largely by high money rates. Call money rates in 1892 were up as high as 35 per cent and in 1893 as high as 15 per cent. Business failures were numerous due to low prices of commodities, principally wheat, corn, and cotton. The 1896 panic was due to the Bryan Silver scare and the fear that the gold standard would be disturbed. However, the low price of commodities had much to do with bringing about this panic, as general business conditions were poor and had been for several years. Call money rates reached 125 per cent, the highest rate up to that time since the Civil War. Average price for stocks reached extreme low on August 8, from which they started up, and after the election of McKinley, the McKinley boom followed, which was the biggest stock boom in this country up to that time. The 1901 panic occurred on the Stock Exchange on May 9, which was due to the Northern Pacific corner.

While stocks rallied after this panic, the general list continued to work lower for several years. In 1903 and 1904, the period of depression was due primarily to undigested securities and to Government attacks upon the railroads. Call money rates reached 15 per cent in 1903 and went back as low as 1 per cent in 1904, and did not get higher than 6 per cent during the year. Business conditions again improved in the latter part of 1904, after the election of Roosevelt, and a bull market followed in 1905 and 1906 when stock market prices reached the highest since the McKinley boom started. The 1907 panic, known as the "rich man's panic," was due to high money rates, overspeculation, trust-busting and to the use of the "big stick" by the late Theodore Roosevelt and legislation against the railroads. Call money went as high as 125 per cent in October 1907, when the panic was at its height. Banks were forced to suspend payment of currency all over the country. The 1910-1911 panic or period of depression was caused primarily by the Sherman Anti-Trust Act and was known as a period of trust-busting.

The Standard Oil Company was ordered to dissolve and a suit brought to dissolve United States Steel Corporation, which later failed. Call money rates reached a high of 12 per cent in 1910. Stock prices reached the lowest levels in July. Money conditions were easier in 1911, the call rate failing to get above 6 per cent. The 1914 panic, which resulted in the closing of the New York Stock Exchange from July 31 to December 15, was due to the outbreak of the World War, but there would have been a panic and business depression in this country if war had not broken out, because commodity prices had reached the lowest levels for many years and business conditions were generally poor. Money rates had been high in 1912, call money reaching 20 per cent and getting as high as 10 per cent in 1913 and 1914. Europe was a large holder of our stocks at the outbreak of the World War and it was this liquidation that forced the New York Stock Exchange to close. Money and business flowed into this country as a result of this war and commodity prices advanced, which helped business here and a boom followed.

Market prices reached high in the Fall of 1916; speculation was overdone and call money reached a high of 15 per cent. Liquidation started, which resulted in the panic of 1917. This was due to over speculation, resulting from the war boom. After the war was over another wild wave of speculation broke out in this country in 1919, culminating in November, and was followed by a panicky decline. Money rates were as high as 30 per cent in October and November 1919, and 25 per cent in the Fall of 1920. The panic of 1920 and 1921 was due principally to "frozen loans" and decline in commodity prices. Merchants all over the country were loaded up with goods bought at high prices and banks were loaded up with loans.

After the panic of 1921 a long period of prosperity followed. Call money did not get above 6 per cent at any time from 1922 until 1928, and during 1924 and 1925 call money rates were down as low as 2 per cent. 1923 and 1924 cannot be considered as panic years either in Wall Street or in the stock market. They were simply periods of reaction, or resting periods, from which the big stock boom was resumed. Business conditions steadily improved after the election of Mr. Coolidge in November 1924. A long period of easy money and expansion in business helped to bring about the greatest bull campaign in stock market history, lasting for the longest period of time of any since the bull campaign which culminated in September 1869, and the McKinley boom from 1898 to 1906.

1929 Wall Street Panic - The cause of this panic was due to wild gambling not only by the people in the United States, but by people in the foreign countries. The whole world was gambling in the stocks of the United States. People were buying right and left regardless of price. Fortunes were made on paper in a short period of time. Everybody from the chambermaid to the multi-millionaire was in the stock market. People had ceased to work and were watching the stock ticker. New millionaires were being made in a short time. People had neglected their business because they thought it was easier to make money in the stock market. Never was there a time before in history where a speculative wave was more overdone than this one. Brokers' loans continued to mount until they reached over 8 billion dollars. It has been conservatively estimated that the total loans on all stocks outstanding in the United States exceeded 30 billions of dollars. At the top, when high prices were reached, the total value of all stocks traded in on the New York Stock Exchange exceeded 100 billion dollars. Bond prices started to decline in 1928 and money rates started to advance, which was the first warning that the bull campaign was nearing its end. Call money rates were as high as 13 per cent in 1928 and went to 20 per cent in 1929. Warnings issued by the Federal Reserve Bank went unheeded.

The largest number of new securities were floated in 1929 of any year in the history of the New York Stock Exchange, all of which required large amounts of money to finance. The last stage of this greatest bull market had been so rapid that a reaction, an orderly decline, or an orderly wave of liquidation was impossible. When everybody had bought to capacity and started to sell, there was no one else who wanted to buy and a collapse was inevitable. The decline was the greatest in history and the public suffered the greatest losses. However, this was a rich man's panic as well as the poor man's, and the multi-millionaire suffered along with the "lamb." Profits of 5, 10, 25, and 100 million or more were wiped out in the short period of less than 3 months. The big traders were just as unable to get out of stocks as the little fellow, because there was no one to buy the stocks that they had to sell. On September 3, the day that the market averages reached extreme high, sales were around 4½ million shares; then when the decline started on September 5, sales were around 5½ million shares. They had not been running above the 5 million-share mark for some time before the market reached top. On October 4, which was the bottom of a reaction, sales were 5½ million. On the first big panic day, October 24, sales were 12,894,000 shares; on October 29, the day of the greatest panic, sales were 16,410,000; on October 28, sales were 9,112,000; on October 30, 10,727,000; on November 12 sales were 6,452,000, and on November 13, the day averages reached bottom, sales were 7,761,000 shares. After this bottom, sales did not exceed 5½ million shares until April 3, when they reached near the 6 million-share mark again.

It is interesting to note the movement on averages from September 3, when the Dow-Jones 30 Industrials reached the high of 381, to October 4, the bottom of the first decline when Averages reached 325, a decline of 56 points in 30 days. A quick rally followed to 363 on October 11, up 38 points. On October 29, the Averages declined to 231, down 132 points from October 11 and 150 points from September 3; after a 2-day rally, Averages reached 273, up 42 points. On November 13 made extreme low at 199, down 74 points from October 31 and 181 points from the top of September 3. A rally followed to December 9, carrying the Averages to 263, up 64 points from the bottom. Then followed a decline to December 20, when the Averages reached 231, down 32 points from December 9. After that the reactions were small and prices worked higher from every reaction until April 17, 1930, when the Averages reached 294, up 95 points from the extreme low made on November 13, 1929.

HOW CYCLES REPEAT

The 1929 stock market panic was due largely to money conditions brought about by overextended loans and undigested securities. A study of conditions following the Civil War and a review of stock market prices will show any man that the conditions which have existed since the great World War have not been vastly different, nor has the stock market been vastly different. Before this bull market ended last August, talk was heard in every part of the country that this bull market had lasted longer than any in history and had fooled the wisest and best of men. The fact that it fooled everybody was

13

true, but the fact that it had lasted longer than any other bull campaign was not wholly true, as the following review of past market movements will prove.

Railroad Averages - I have made up an average on railroad stocks from 1856 to 1896 in order that you may see where prices were before the Civil War started and what happened after the Civil War. In comparing conditions before and after wars, the best barometer and guide is the stock market. A bull campaign culminated in 1856 when these averages reached 96. A panic followed in 1857, carrying these same averages down to a low of 37. In 1858 the high was 79 and the low 59. In 1859 the high was 70 and the low 53. In 1860 the high was 70, the same as in 1859, and the low was 54, one point higher than 1859 low. In 1861 the high was 65 and in March the lowest record was made with the price down to 48. War was declared in April 1861, but you can see that stock market prices had discounted the war and started to advance soon afterwards. In June 1862, the averages crossed 70, which was the high level in 1859 and 1860, and in September crossed 79, the last high which was made in 1858. The bull campaign continued and in January 1863, the averages crossed the high level of 1856. The up trend continued to April 1864, when top was reached at 154. A fast decline followed and in March 1865, the low was again reached at 88, down 66 points in one year's time. In October 1865, the averages rallied to 121. In February 1866, declined to 100. Advanced to 125 in October 1866, then followed a decline which culminated in April 1867, when the low was 104. This was a higher bottom than the low of 1866. From this low another big advance started and the final high was reached in July 1869, when the averages were top at 181, up 77 points from the low of April 1867. The last stage of the 1869 Bull Campaign was wild and active, with an advance of about 33 points on averages in the last three months of this final grand rush.

The bull campaign, which really began in March 1861, lasted until July 1869, subject to reactions just the same as we had in the bull campaign from 1921 to August 1929. The bull campaign from 1861 to 1869 was 8 years and 4 months. The bull campaign from August 1921, to August 1929, lasted 8 years. You can see by the records previous to the Civil War and following the Civil War that the bull campaign at that time lasted slightly longer than the bull campaign from 1921 to 1929.

A decline started in August 1869, and the real panic took place in September, and a "Black Friday" occurred on September 24, 1869. The stock Averages declined 30 points during the month of September, reaching a low of 144. In October a quick rally followed, making high of 167. This was the last high and stocks started working lower with nothing but small rallies until the panic of 1873, when the averages sold at 84, down 97 points from the high of July 1869. A rally followed which culminated in February 1874, the averages reaching 107. In September 1874, they declined to 95; rallied to 106 in May 1875; and again declined to 95 in October 1875. In March 1876, the averages again rallied to 110. A decline followed to December 1876, when the low recorded was 81, down 100 points from the high of July 1869. After this a bull campaign followed, lasting until November 1879, when the averages reached 119. Another decline set in, which culminated in June 1880, with the averages down to 73. From this low level, a sharp advance followed culminating in January 1881, with the high at 118, just one point under the high of November 1879. In May and June 1881, the averages made the same high level again. From this top, a long bear campaign followed to June 1884, when the low reached was 51. In August, there was a rally to 72 and in March, May, and June 1885, the averages reached bottom at 52, one point higher than the extreme low of the previous year. In November 1885, the averages rallied again to 73 and in May 1886, again declined to 53, which was the last low. From this low level, a creeping bull market started which gradually worked higher until May 1890, when the averages reached 89. A bear campaign followed which resulted in the panic of

1893, the bottom being reached in July with the averages down to 61. This same low was again recorded in December 1893. An advance followed which culminated in September 1895, with the averages at 106. From this top the Bryan Silver panic, which culminated in 1896, followed. On August 8, 1896, stocks reached the lowest level which they had recorded since the Civil War, or the lowest since July 1869, when top was made after the Civil War. In 1896 many stocks went into the hands of receivers. Stocks like New York Central, which made high in 1869, continued to work lower until bottom was reached in 1896.

From 1896 to date the Dow-Jones Averages on Railroad and Industrial stocks are the most reliable guides to the trend of the market. These Averages were reviewed in TRUTH OF THE STOCK TAPE from 1896 to 1922. In 1928, when they crossed the high level of 1906, which was the highest price in history, you should then have looked up the high prices of the individual stocks which made up this group of averages and noted the ones that had crossed the high level of 1906. For example: Atchison, New York Central, and Union Pacific, which crossed the 1906 tops, were among the rails which made the biggest advances, while St. Paul and other stocks, which did not reach this level, advanced very little compared to the advances in Atchison, New York Central and Union Pacific.

It is well for traders to know these things and to know that what has happened in the past can happen again. You should never hold on and hope. When you see that you are wrong, place a stop loss order or get out and take a quick loss. Hundreds of thousands of people were fooled in the bull market which culminated in 1929, and hundreds of thousands will be fooled before many stocks which were top in 1929 will reach bottom. The only way to protect yourself against heavy losses is to get out before it is too late. Stubbornness will not help in the stock market. In fact, nothing helps you when you are wrong, except to get out and wait for another opportunity or to get right on some other stock.

SECTIONS OF A BULL CAMPAIGN

A bull market, as a rule, moves in sections or waves. The campaign from 1921 to 1929 moved in sections as follows: The bottom for the Dow-Jones 20 Industrial Stock Averages was reached in August 1921, and the move started up. The first section of the bull campaign culminated in March 1923. Then there was a reaction or a small bear campaign. Some stocks made bottom in May 1924, and others made bottom in October 1924. From this reaction in a bull market, the second section of the bull campaign started and the advance continued until November 1925, but this was only a reaction in a bull market. The bull campaign was resumed and the third section of the advance lasted from April to August 1926; then there was a two months' reaction to October 1926, from which the upswing was again resumed. In October 1927, top was made for another quick, sharp reaction, but it only lasted for one month. However, many stocks rested and reacted until February 1928, when they started up again and there was a fast advance culminating in January and February 1929. This can be considered the end of the third section of the bull campaign. A panicky decline followed in March and low levels were reached on March 26, 1929. Stocks held in a narrow, trading range or accumulated for about two months. The fourth or last section of the bull campaign started in May 1929. This was the final grand rush. Many stocks made the biggest advance of any time in history in the same period of time. From May until September 3, 1929, the Averages of the Dow-Jones 30 Industrial stocks went up 90 points. From the culmination of this bull campaign, which was made with only a few active, high-priced stocks, in which big traders were operating, a great deluge followed and in a little over two months' time, the Averages declined 182 points, the biggest decline in history with the greatest losses to the public and pool operators that had ever been recorded. The total loss in quoted values was over 40 billion dollars.

Industrial Averages - This group of Dow-Jones Averages was reviewed from 1896 to 1922 and a monthly and a yearly high and low chart shown in TRUTH OF THE STOCK TAPE. The high in October 1922, was 103 and the low in November 1922, was 92. From this low level an advance followed which culminated in March 1923, when the Averages reached 105, only 2 points above the 1922 high and still 4 points under the 1920 high, which level they would have to cross to indicate higher prices. A decline followed and in October 1923, the Averages reached a low of 86. Around this level there was big accumulation, holding in a range from 86 to 88 for 5 months. A rally followed and in January and February 1924, reached a high of 100. Then declined to May 1924, making a low of 88½, where the Averages held for 3 months, making the same low level each month. This was 2 points above the 1923 low level, which showed good support and indicated that stocks were going higher. August 1924, high 105, same high as March 1923. A moderate reaction followed to October 1924 when the low reached was 100. There was a rally at the end of this month and the Averages closed at 104 and in November opened at 104 and quickly crossed 105, the highest level for over 2 years, a sure indication for much higher prices. At this time you should have selected the stocks in the strongest position in this group and should have bought them to hold for the long pull.

After the election of Mr. Coolidge in November 1924, stocks started to advance rapidly and before the end of November the Averages had crossed 109, the high of 1920, another good sign for much higher prices. The next high point was 120, the high of 1919, which was the highest in history. This level was crossed in December 1924, another good indication of a big advance to follow. March 1925, high 125; a quick decline followed and late in March the low reached was 115. Here there was good support and prices started to move up again. In May the Averages crossed the March high of 125 and each month the bottoms and tops were higher until February 1926, when the Averages reached a high of 162. This was a sharp top, and a sharp, quick decline followed in March when there was really a panicky break, many of the active stocks declining 75 to 100 points. The low on the Averages was 135. This was only one month's reaction, the same as March 1925. The market held in a dull, narrow range for about 2 months while accumulation was taking place and in June the main trend turned up again. August 1926, the averages reached a high of 166, just 4 points above the January 1926 high, but an indication that they were going higher later. A quick decline followed lasting nearly 2 months, getting down to a low of 146 in October 1926. The advance was resumed, big accumulation showing in the active leaders, and in May 1927, the Averages crossed 166, another indication for much higher prices and in October reached a high of 199. Good selling always appears around the even figures, like 100, 200 and 300. A decline quickly followed and before the end of the month the Averages had declined to 179. But a rapid advance followed this break. In January 1928, the Averages crossed 200. Getting above the even figure was a sure sign for much higher prices. They made 203; then had a small reaction in February, making a low of 192, and in March a rapid advance started and prices crossed 203. Top was reached in May and June 1928, when the price was 220. A quick decline followed to 202 in June. The Averages failing to break the even figure of 200 showed good support and indicated higher prices. There was a big accumulation in July and in August a wild, runaway market started and continued until February 1929, when the Averages made a high of 222. A decline followed in March and the Averages reached 196. Then followed a sharp, quick advance and in April the Averages made a new high at 227. A decline started in the early part of May from a sharp top and there was a sharp decline down to a low of 194 in the latter part of May, holding just 2 points under the low of March 1929, a good indication of bottom. In June a rapid advance started with public utilities and late movers leading this advance.

The Averages continued to work higher each month, making higher bottoms and higher tops until September 3, 1929, when the final top was reached with the Averages at 381, the highest price in history. This was a sharp top made on heavy volume of sales in most of the active stocks. A quick, sharp decline followed. September 5, low 370, followed by a quick rally on September 7 to a high of 377, making a lower top; September 9 declined to 367, a sign of weakness and an indication for much lower prices; September 11 a quick rally to 371; September 12 a low of 366½, another sign of weakness; September 16 rallied to 372, failing to get much above the last high level; September 19 broke 366, a sign that the big decline was on; October 4 reached a low of 326; a sharp rally followed to October 11, when top was made at 362, making lower top than the previous one. From this top a panicky decline took place and on October 29 the low reached was 231. A fast rally, lasting only 2 days, followed to October 31, making a high of 273. Liquidation broke out again and a sharp decline followed, reaching final bottom November 13, when the averages made a low of 199, down 182 points from the high of September 3, 1929.

This was the fastest decline ever recorded, and will go down in history as Wall Street's greatest panic. A rapid recovery followed to December 9 when the high was 263. Then followed a decline to December 20, reaching a low of 231. Note that the low for the Averages on October 29 and on December 20, were at the same level, being 32 points higher than the extreme low made in November, 1929. This was a sign for higher prices later. From this bottom a slow advance followed with only small reactions. On February 5 and 14, 1930, the Averages made temporary top at 272; then declined to February 24, making a low of 263. The advance was resumed and on April 17, reached a high of 294.

The Dow-Jones 30 Industrial Averages are a good guide to the trend of the active stocks in this list, but remember that you must study the individual stocks and see if they conform to the change in trend of the Averages. If a stock shows opposite trend, play it that way. Watch the Averages when they get dull and narrow and see if the volume is very small at the bottom or the top, which is a sign for a change. Then watch when the market is very active at bottom and top and see if the volume increases right along. As soon as the volume begins to show a decrease, then look for a change in trend and a reverse move to follow.

CHAPTER II
TWENTY-FOUR NEVER-FAILING RULES

In order to make a success trading in the stock market, the trader must have definite rules and follow them. The rules given below are based upon my personal experience and anyone who follows them will make a success.

1. Amount of capital to use: Divide your capital into 10 equal parts and never risk more than one-tenth of your capital on any one trade.

2. Use stop loss orders. Always protect a trade when you make it with a stop loss order 3 to 5 points away.

3. Never over trade. This would be violating your capital rule.

4. Never let a profit run into a loss. After you once have a profit of 3 points or more, raise your stop loss order so that you will have no loss of capital.

5. Do not buck the trend. Never buy or sell if you are not sure of the trend according to your charts.

6. When in doubt, get out, and don't get in when in doubt.

7. Trade only in active stocks. Keep out of slow, dead ones.

8. Equal distribution of risk. Trade in 4 or 5 stocks, if possible. Avoid tying up all your capital in any one stock.

9. Never limit your orders or fix a buying or selling price. Trade at the market.

10. Don't close your trades without a good reason. Follow up with a stop loss order to protect your profits.

11. Accumulate a surplus. After you have made a series of successful trades, put some money into surplus account to be used only in emergency or in times of panic.

12. Never buy just to get a dividend.

13. Never average a loss. This is one of the worst mistakes a trader can make.

14 Never get out of the market just because you have lost patience or get into the market because you are anxious from waiting.

15. Avoid taking small profits and big losses.

16. Never cancel a stop loss order after you have placed it at the time you make a trade.

17. Avoid getting in and out of the market too often.

18. Be just as willing to sell short as you are to buy. Let your object be to keep with the trend and make money.

19. Never buy just because the price of a stock is low or sell short just because the price is high.

20. Be careful about pyramiding at the wrong time. Wait until the stock is very active and has crossed Resistance Levels before buying more and until it has broken out of the zone of distribution before selling more.

21. Select the stocks with small volume of shares outstanding to pyramid on the buying side and the ones with the largest volume of stock outstanding to sell short.

22. Never hedge. If you are long of one stock and it starts to go down, do not sell another stock short to hedge it. Get out at the market; take your loss and wait for another opportunity.

23. Never change your position in the market without a good reason. When you make a trade, let it be for some good reason or according to some definite plan; then do not get out without a definite indication of a change in trend.

24. Avoid increasing your trading after a long period of success or a period of profitable trades.

When you decide to make a trade, be sure that you are not violating any of these 24 rules, which are vital and important to your success. When you close a trade with a loss, go over these rules and see which rule you have violated; then do not make the same mistake the second time. Experience and investigation will convince you of the value of these rules, and observation and study will lead you to a correct and practical theory for success in Wall Street.

SAFETY OF CAPITAL

Your first thought must be how to protect your capital and make your trading as safe as possible. There is one safe, sure rule, and the man who will follow it and never deviate from it will always keep his money and come out ahead at the end of every year. This rule is divide your capital into 10 equal parts and never risk more than one-tenth or 10 per cent of your capital on any one trade. If you start with $1000 you should not risk more than $100 on your first trade, and the way to limit your loss is to place a stop loss order. It is much better to have 10 shares of stock and lose 3 points or $30 than to have 100 shares and lose $300. You can always find new opportunities to make profits, so long as you have capital to operate with. Taking heavy risks in the beginning endangers your capital and impairs your judgment. Trade in such a way that you will not be disturbed mentally by a loss, if it comes.

STOP LOSS ORDERS

I feel that I cannot repeat too many times the value of using stop loss orders because it is the only safety valve to protect the investor and trader. An investor or trader will place a stop loss order and one time out of ten the stop will be caught at the exact top or bottom. After this he always remembers that and says, "If I place a stop loss order, they will just go down and catch it, or just go up and catch it and then the market will go the other way." So he does not use the stop loss order the next time. His broker often tells him that stop loss orders are always caught. The trader forgets that nine times out of ten the stop loss order was right and would have prevented big losses by getting him out at a time when the market was going against him. The one time that the stop loss order gets you out wrong it makes up for it in the next nine times that it gets you out right. So don't fail to use a stop loss order.

CHANGING YOUR MIND

A wise man changes his mind, a fool never. A wise man investigates and then decides, and a fool just decides. In Wall Street, the man who does not change his mind will soon have no change to mind. When once you have made up your mind to make a trade and you have a reason for it, do not change without a reason. The most important thing that I refer to is changing stop loss orders, or canceling stops when the market is going against you. The first thing to do when you make a trade is to place a stop loss order, which is for your own protection. Once you have placed a stop, you have acted wisely and used good judgment. To change your mind from this decision is foolish and to cancel your stop, once you have placed it, is not based on good judgment but on hope, and hope can lead to nothing but losses in Wall Street. Nine times out of ten, when once you place a stop loss order, if you never cancel it, it will prove to be the best thing that ever happened, and the man who adheres to this rule will make a success. I reiterate, if you cannot follow a rule, do not start to speculate because you will lose all, and one of the rules that you must follow and never deviate from is to PLACE A STOP LOSS ORDER AT THE TIME YOU MAKE A TRADE AND DO NOT CANCEL IT.

OVERTRADING

History repeats because of the weakness of human nature. The greed for quick fortunes has cost the public countless millions of dollars. Every experienced stock trader knows that overtrading is his greatest weakness, but he continues to allow this weakness to be his ruin. There must be a cure for this greatest weakness in trading, and that cure is STOP LOSS ORDERS. The weakest point must be overcome, and the stop loss order is the cure for overtrading.

PROTECT YOUR PROFITS

It is just as important to protect profits, as it is to protect your capital. When once you have a profit on a trade, you should never let it run into a loss. There are exceptions to this rule, and the amount of the profits should determine where stop loss orders should be placed. The following is about the safest rule that I can give you to use under average conditions. When once a stock has moved 3 points in your favor, place a stop loss order where you will be even if it is caught. In very active, high-priced stocks, it will pay you to wait until a stock shows a profit of 4 to 5 points; then move your stop loss order up to where you will have no loss should the market reverse. In this way, you will have reduced your risk to a minimum and the possibility of profits will be unlimited. As the stock moves in your favor, continue to follow up with a stop loss order, thus protecting and increasing your profits.

WHEN TO ENTER THE MARKET

It is very important to know when to buy or sell, and you must have some rule or some sign as your indication for the time to place your order to buy or sell. When you think the market is reaching bottom or top, you will find that 7 times out of 10 you will be wrong. It is not what the market does today or what you think it is going to do that is important; it is exactly what the indications are that it will do at a later date when you expect to make profits.

When a stock reaches low levels or high levels and you want to take a position, wait until it shows a sign that the trend has turned up or down. At times, you may miss the bottom or top by waiting, but you will save money by not making your trade until you have reason to believe that you are going with the trend and not against it.

One of the most important things that you should keep in mind is not how much profit or how much loss you are going to make. You should leave the money part out of the question. Your object should be to keep right on the market. Go with the trend of the market. Study all the time to determine the correct trend. Do not think about profits. If you are right on the market, the profits will come. If you are wrong, then use the old reliable protector, a stop loss order.

BUYING OR SELLING TOO SOON OR TOO LATE

Investors often get out of the market too soon, because they have held stocks for a long time, waiting for activity and higher prices, and then sell out on the first move up into new territory, which is a mistake.

There is another type of investor who always gets out of the market too late, because when the big advance comes, he holds on and hopes that the stock will go higher than it ever does. It never reaches the price at which he wishes to sell. The first quick break comes, and he decides that if the stock advances again to its former high level, he will sell out. The stock does advance but fails to get as high, then declines still lower, and he again fixes a price in his mind at which he will sell, but this is only a "hope" price, and he sees the stock drift lower and lower until finally, in disgust, he sells out after the stock has had a big decline from the top. It is always well to wait until you can see a change in the trend before selling out, but when once you do see that the trend has changed, then sell out without delay. A good rule for this kind of a trader is to follow up with stop loss orders, even if it is 10 to 20 points away.

DELAYS DANGEROUS

Action, not delay, makes money in Wall Street. There is no use hoping, as that will not beat the game. Men who gamble on hope always go broke. You must stop hoping and start thinking. Then, after you think, unless you act at the proper time, good thinking is useless. Knowing when to act and not doing it will not help any. Delays are always dangerous. The longer you hope and delay taking action in the market, the worse your judgment gets and the surer you are to make mistakes. Stagnation is death and destruction. Action is life. Being right or wrong and not acting will never save your money or help you to make it. Remember, delays are always dangerous. It is much better to take action now than to trust to uncertain time. You should never trade when sick or depressed. Your judgment is always bad when you are below normal physically. One of the rules of a successful speculator should be to keep good health, for health is wealth.

WHEN TO PYRAMID

There are two ways of pyramiding. One is to buy more or sell more just as soon as the market breaks into new territory or makes a new high or a new low. In a fast running market, you can continue to buy or sell every 3, 5 or 10 points up or down when the market is moving in your favor, all depending on the stock or your method of pyramiding. My method is to determine the reaction levels and how many points a stock has reacted from temporary top levels or rallied from temporary bottoms. Find out whether these reactions are running 3, 5, 7, 10, or 12 points; then buy or sell your 1st, 2nd, 3rd, or 4th lot for pyramiding on reactions from the top, waiting for 3, 8, or 10 points according to the past reaction. Reverse the rule in a bear market. If you had followed this rule on General Motors from 1924 to 1929, you would find that your pyramid would have been safer than buying or selling the stock every so many points apart.

My time rule, which will help you in pyramiding, is to determine the time of the first important reaction. For example, General Motors reacted only 3 weeks from the time it started up in 1924 and was good to buy every time it reacted 2 to 3 weeks from any top, until it made the final top and the main trend turned down. Determining the time of the reactions and measuring them this way will greatly increase your profits and enable you to follow the main trend of the stock, sometimes for several years, and you can often make 100 to 200 points profit. This time rule, like other rules, works best on active high-priced stocks and should only be applied in active markets.

A pyramid should always be followed up with a stop loss order, no matter what method you use, because your profits must be protected. The more profit you have, the more room you can give the market to fluctuate, or have its reverse moves or reactions, that is, you can place your stop loss order further away from the market so that a natural reaction will not disturb your pyramid. For example, suppose you have followed a stock up and have 100 points profit on your original purchase. If the stock has had a previous reaction of 20 points, it could again react 20 points without changing the main trend, therefore your stop loss order could be 20 points under the market, because if it was caught, you would not be losing part of your capital, but only a part of your paper profits, while in the early stages of your pyramid your stop loss order would have to be closer in order to protect your original capital.

HOW MUCH PROFIT TO EXPECT

Most traders expect too large profits from the business of speculation. They do not stop to figure what a gain of 25 per cent a year means over a period of 10 to 20 years. Starting with $1000 a gain of 25 per cent per year for 10 years equals $9,313.25. $10,000 increased at the rate of 25 per cent a year amounts to $93,132.70 in 10 years. You can see how easy it is to accumulate a fortune in a reasonable length of time if one only is conservative and does not expect too much. Many traders come to Wall Street with the idea that they can double their money in a week or a month. It cannot be done. There are exceptional opportunities at times, when a large amount of money can be made in one day, one week, or one month, but these big opportunities are few and far between, and when once you have one of them and make big profits, do not let hope run away with your judgment and expect to continue to make profits right along on such an enormous scale. Remember that the market makes normal moves most of the time and that you must take normal profits the greater part of the time.

Many traders buy or sell a stock without any thought of how much profit there is a possibility of them making and never think about the possibility of a loss. This should be one of your rules: Never buy or sell a stock when you don't think you can make more than 3 to 5 points' profit unless you use a stop loss order of only 1 to 2 points. It does not pay, on an average, to risk 3 to 5 points' loss for a possible gain of 3 to 5 points. Try to make a trade where you have opportunities, or at least where there is a promise of greater profits than losses. There is no use getting into a stock when you think there is only a chance of making 3 to 5 points, because you can be wrong and lose that much or more. It is better to wait until stocks cross Resistance Levels one way or the other and get in where the opportunities are for greater profits and longer swings. Scalpers do not make money; they simply get scalped. Remember that to make a success your profits must always be greater than your losses, and your rule must be to cut losses short and let your profits run.

HOW TO ANSWER A MARGIN CALL

When you make a trade and put up the required margin at the time and later the stock goes against you and the broker calls for more margin, the thing to do in most cases is not to put up more margin, but sell out at the market or buy in, in case you are short. If you put up more margin, let it be on a new trade and one which you have a good reason for making when your judgment is better. Nine times out of ten after a customer puts up margin the first time, he will hold on until there is a second margin call and a third and put up as long as he has money to put up and lose all of his capital on one trade. If the broker has to call you for margin, there is something wrong, and the best thing to do is to get out.

JOINT ACCOUNTS

Never have a joint account or trade in partnership with others if you can possibly avoid it. When two men have an account together, they may agree upon the right time to buy for long account or the right time to sell short and may be exactly right when they agree to make the trade, but here is where the hitch comes - when it comes to closing the trade they will seldom ever agree on the time and price to take profits. The result will be that they will make a mistake in getting out of the trade. One man will hold on because the other one does not want to get out and finally the market reverses and the trade goes against them; then they hold on and hope, and finally take a loss on what was a trade that they started together profitably. It is hard for one mind to work on the stock market and keep right, but it is much harder for two to agree and work in the market. The only way that two could make a success with it would be for one to do the buying and selling and the other to do nothing but place the stop loss orders. Stop loss orders will protect both of them when they make mistakes. It is a bad rule for a man and his wife to have a joint account together. The action of getting in and out of the market should be up to one man, who should learn to act and act quickly and not be influenced by a partner in a speculative deal.

The average trader does not want to hear a painful truth. They want something in accordance with what they hope for. When they buy a stock they believe all the news, rumors, views and lies that are bullish, but just let some report come out that is bad or let someone tell him something unfavorable about the stock he has bought and he refuses to believe it. It is the truth that will help him and truth that he should want to hear, not something that will build up his hopes and cause him losses later. A trader after he has made a mistake, says "I am going to do different next time," but he doesn't and that is why we always have old lambs in Wall Street to lead the young lambs down the same lane to losses that the old lambs have followed. Real inside truth about losses in Wall Street is seldom ever told.

Traders, big and little, always talk about their profits and brag about their successful trades, but keep quiet about their losses. Therefore, the innocent lamb, when he comes to Wall Street, is led to believe that there is nothing but profits to be made, instead of hearing the other side of the story of how losses are made in Wall Street, which is a thing that would really help him and prevent him from making the same mistake. The new lamb should know that failing to place a stop loss order and overtrading have been the cause of over 90 per cent of the failures in Wall Street. Therefore, in order to make a success he must act in a way to overcome the weak points which have caused the ruin of others.

HUMAN ELEMENT THE GREATEST WEAKNESS

When a trader makes a profit, he gives himself credit and feels that his judgment is good and that he did it all himself. When he makes losses, he takes a different attitude and seldom ever blames himself or tries to find the cause with himself for the losses. He finds excuses; reasons with himself that the unexpected happened, and that if he had not listened to some one else's advice, he would have made a profit He finds a lot of ifs, ands, and buts, which he imagines were no fault of his. This is why he makes mistakes and losses the second time.

The investor and trader must work out his own salvation and blame himself and no one else for his losses, for unless he does, he will never be able to correct his weaknesses. After all, it is your own acts that cause your losses, because you did the buying and the selling. You must look for the trouble within and correct it. Then you will make a success, and not before.

One of the main reasons why traders make losses is because they do not think for themselves and allow others to think for them and advise them, whose advice and judgment is no better than their own. To make a success, you must study and investigate for yourself. Unless you change from a "lamb" to a thinker and seek knowledge, you will go the way of all lambs - to slaughter under the margin caller's axe. Others can only help you when you help yourself, or show you how to help yourself.

I can give you the best rules in the world and the best methods for determining the position of a stock, and then you can lose money on account of the human element, which is your greatest weakness. You will fail to follow rules. You will work on hope or fear instead of facts. You will delay. You will become impatient. You will act too quickly or you will delay too long in acting, thus cheating yourself on account of your human weakness and then blaming it on the market. Always remember that it is your mistake that causes losses and not the action of the market or the manipulators. Therefore, strive to follow rules, or keep out of speculation for you are doomed to failure.

CHAPTER III
WALL STREET EDUCATION

WHY IT IS HARDER TO BEAT THE STOCK MARKET NOW

Every year it gets more difficult for the average trader to make money in the stock market, because the number of stocks increases. There are about 1500 stocks listed on the New York Stock Exchange. Opposite moves are more numerous than ever before. Stocks in the same group will move in opposite directions. One stock in **a** group declining or advancing in opposition to the general trend will cause a trader to become confused and make mistakes.

When the number of active stocks listed was very small and most of them contained in the Dow-Jones Industrials and Rails, these Averages were a reliable guide. Then stocks were in the hands of a few large holders, and manipulators moved these groups of stocks most all at the same time. The large number of stocks now listed on the Stock Exchange compose so many different groups that in order to get a reliable guide on averages, one has to have the averages of the different groups, such as, oils, rubbers, steels, manufacturing stocks, etc. You must not give too much weight to the averages, but should determine the position of each individual stock which composes these averages. You will find some stocks in a very weak position and showing down trend and at the same time other stocks in the group in a very strong position, as we will show under the analyses of stocks in the different groups.

The law of averages works when applied to life insurance. The actuary can figure the lives of 1000 men at various ages and tell on an average how many of them will die each year, but the actuary cannot figure on one individual and tell when he will die from the position of the average because of the fact that men born at different times are grouped under the same average. Stock averages are also made up of stocks from companies which are 5, 10, 20, 30, 50, and 100 years old. With such a wide difference in the time of the incorporation, and with the industries located in different parts of the country and influenced by local as well as other conditions, it is only natural that some of them must go opposite to the trend of the average group.

For example: Take the oil industry and the group of oil stocks which make up the averages. The companies which compose these averages were formed at different times, managed by different men, their offices located in different parts of the country and subject to the various conditions. Therefore, in order to get a reliable Forecast, each company and its stock must be analyzed separately, judged and forecast individually and not collectively. An example of this was the time when Houston Oil had a big advance at the same time other oil stocks were declining. There was a very small supply of Houston Oil and its position was different and it was easy to put it up against the trend of the general list.

In order to make a success trading in stocks under present conditions, a trader must study each individual stock and follow it according to its own trend, regardless of the action of the stocks in the same group or the action of the general market or any other single stock or group of stocks. With the weakness of human nature, this is hard to do and makes it all the more necessary for a trader to have fixed rules and strictly adhere to them, and the one rule that he must always use is to place a stop loss order.

This country has grown so large and is doing business with so many of the foreign countries that changed conditions and events, favorable or unfavorable, happening in foreign countries, affect our markets and make it harder for the trader who just guesses, follows tips or inside information. The truth is that he simply cannot beat the market this way.

This country has changed from an agricultural to a manufacturing nation. There was a time when railroad stocks followed the crops. If the crops were good, railroad stocks would advance. Short crops would cause a decline. When the railroads no longer had to depend upon crops for their tonnage but received a large part of their business from the manufacturing concerns, then the man who used crops as an indicator for rails found his guide unreliable.

Conditions now change rapidly in this country. The modes of transportation from Fulton's steamboat to the railroad were a long way apart, but from the beginning of the use of automobiles for pleasure and commercial purposes to the use of the airplane was a much shorter period of time. The automobile changed conditions for the railroads, and now the airplane will change conditions for the automobile industry as well as railroads. This is plainly shown by the fact that large automobile concerns are all trying to get into the business of manufacturing airplanes, because it is the coming mode of transportation and the companies that continue to manufacture automobiles alone will find their business and earnings decreasing in the years to come.

To make a success, you must keep ahead of the times and not behind them. You must watch for the best stocks in the new industries. Do not hold on to old stocks and hope for them to come back. When they start on the downward trend, sell them short, just as the man should have played the short side of railroad stocks from 1909 to 1917, and then, when the change came in 1921 and railroad stocks showed up trend, he could have made money buying them. The industrial stocks have shown greater opportunities and bigger profits than the rails, in most cases, during the period of the world's greatest bull market.

AGE AT WHICH A MAN CAN TAKE SPECULATIVE RISKS

From the time a man is 20 years old on up to 50, he has to take certain chances in order to make large amounts of money, but these chances or risks must be based on sound judgment or some science in selecting the stocks to make investments or speculative purchases. By the time a man reaches the age of 50 he should be independent. If he has followed any rules for success in speculation or investments, he should be in a position where it is not necessary to take risks or heavy chances. If he is not in this position, he should not take chances anyway because the average proves that after a man reaches 50 and loses his money or goes broke in business, he seldom comes back again. If he is a failure in Wall Street at 50, he had better quit. If he is a success at that age, he does not have to worry and should take it easy in the future. It is a human weakness and only natural to risk part of the money which is left after big losses in order to get back the money lost. This is a great mistake that many men make who speculate or go into business ventures after the age of 50. Of course, there are exceptions to all rules. Some men make a success after 60, a few after 70, but we are speaking of the average. To make a success in speculation or in business, around the age of 20 a man should begin to

28

study a business or the stock market and gain knowledge and experience. If he puts in 10 years of study up to 30, he will be at that time prepared to make a success in speculation during the next 10 or 20 years, but if he quits studying at 30 after he thinks he knows enough to make a success, he will be a failure at some time during the next 20 years.

He must continue to study changed conditions in the market and the position of new stocks as well as old stocks and not let changed conditions fool him at a different period in the age of a stock. He must not put new wine in old bottles, or, in other words, use his old yardstick for measuring stocks in a different cycle or a different period as many traders did in the bull campaign from 1921 to 1929, especially during the section from 1924 to 1929 when traders thought that the bull campaign had lasted as long as it should compared with previous bull campaigns and made the mistake of going short too soon or selling out longs too soon.

Every man must get his stock market education and must remember that one never graduates from the Wall Street school. You must take post-graduate courses every year to keep up with the times; in fact, keep ahead of the times, in order to make a success in Wall Street.

CAN A MAN LOSE $100,000,000?

The general public has the idea that after a man has one million dollars or more, he cannot lose it. In other words, he is a big fellow and can force the market to go his way. We only have to refer to the case of J. 0. Armour who lost over $300,000,000. At the end of the great World War, Armour, the packing king, possessed a fortune of about $300,000,000. Changed conditions, brought about by the war, caused his fortune to start slipping away. When he saw a loss of $20,000,000 he refused to accept it but fought with the other $280,000,000 to save the $20,000,000. The market continued to go against him, and business got worse instead of better. He continued to buck the trend until his entire fortune was wiped out, his health gone, and he died hopelessly bankrupt. Certainly, he made his fight for the love of money, because he had no use for this amount of money, but once he had it he gave his health and all he had trying to keep it.

W. C. Durant, who was reputed to be worth $120,000,000 at the height of the bull campaign in 1919, lost it all, and his holdings of General Motors were taken over by the Morgans and the du Ponts below the market. There are numbers of instances of men who made anywhere from 5 to 50 million dollars and then lost it all. Daniel Drew was worth about 13 million dollars, according to his own statement, and then lost it all and died broke. Thomas W. Lawson was worth anywhere from 30 to 50 million dollars. He lost it all and died practically penniless. Daniel J. Sully, Eugene Scales, Jesse Livermore, and many others have lost 5 million or more.

In the 1929 panic big traders lost 10, 25, 50, 75, and 100 million and some are reported to have lost 200 to 300 millions in 90 days. If these men can lose millions or hundreds of millions, certainly you have no better chance than they have. When a man with 100 million dollars gets wrong, he can lose it just as easily as a man can lose $100 when he is wrong and much faster. A man with $100 can get out but the man with $100,000,000 cannot. Perhaps you would like to ask why a man with 5, 10, or 100 million dollars loses it all. It is because he does not use the same judgment that he used in making it. It is one thing to make money and another thing to keep it. A man's life runs in cycles just the same as stocks. He reaches his apex and does not know it. His time for moneymaking ends, and he should keep what he has already made, rather than try to make more. There is a seasonal trend and a mathematical, scientific cycle which determines the time and limits to which a man can go, and when he bucks the law and the tide turns against him, he is carried down by the undertow. *The most important thing for every man to know is when to quit.* After a man has made money, he must know when he has enough, stop and keep what he has.

Shrewd traders often make the mistake of following a leader who has been successful. They follow him when he is on the down trend and when his judgment is no better, in fact, not as good as their own. Thousands of people who had followed Durant from 1915 to 1919, when he was right and made millions of dollars, continued to follow him during 1920 and 1921, when he was wrong, and lost everything they had made, and more too. How could they have prevented these losses? By using some method of their own which would determine when the trend of motor stocks had turned down, then stop buying, sell out longs and go short.

Any man who followed my rules for reading charts could see from the position of General Motors and other motor stocks that the trend had turned down in the latter part of 1919 and continued down during 1920 and 1921. Then why should they have followed Durant when he was wrong and lost all of his money? Never pin your faith to any one leader and stick too long. The lone hunter or fisherman is the man who bags the game. When there are too many followers, they help to defeat the purpose of the leader. The big men are just as often wrong as the little fellow, but most of them are smart enough to change quickly when they find they are wrong and do not hold on and hope, as the public does.

WHEN A MAN'S TREND CHANGES

Man's seasonal trend changes just as the market and he has his good and bad cycles. By keeping a record of your own trades, you can determine when your trend is changing one way or the other. I have been able to make as many as 200 consecutive trades without a loss. When I started the campaign, I did not believe I could make 50 trades without a loss, but I did continue to make perfect trades and close every trade with a profit, until I had made 200 trades. This run of luck or up trend that I was in had run for some time. If I had no way to forecast it, what sign should I watch to tell when the tide had turned against me and I should get out and wait? The first indication that something was wrong would be the first trade on which I made a loss. I remember that it was a small loss, around $100. On the next trade I had a loss of over $500. This showed that my trend was changing and turning against me, whether due to bad judgment, ill health, tired nerves, or other causes. If I had been wise, I would have quit and kept all of my profits. I made the third trade and as most traders do, went into the market on a larger scale. This trade soon showed a loss of $5,000 and I did not take the loss quickly. The result was that I continued to make a series of losses until the banks closed in November 1907, and I could not get any more money out of the banks. I was forced to close out all of my commitments with my brokers and take a big loss, because I was bucking my own trend.

My period of good luck had run out, and I was trading in a period which should have been for rest, recreation, and gaining knowledge instead of trying to make more money which I did not need. The banks were unable to pay currency for several months, and I could not get any money to speculate with. I put in my time studying and figuring on the market and found out what caused my mistake and the losses.

I started trading again in the Spring of 1908, and should have had some rule to tell me when my trend had turned in my favor. I began to trade in Wheat and the first three trades I made showed profits. This was a sign that luck was with me and I should press it. I then started a campaign buying Cotton and followed the market right on up, pyramiding at the same time that Livermore made his first successful corner in July Cotton. I made a large amount of money.

I could give you many more examples of my experiences of profits and losses but one rule that every trader should watch and follow is, just as soon as he makes two or three wrong trades after a long series of profits, he should quit the market and take a rest. Get away from the market. Allow plenty of time for his judgment to clear up. Then, when he thinks he is right again, make a start on a small trade. If the first trade goes against him, he should quit again and stay away. Then, when he starts again, if his first two or three trades show profits, he can press his luck and expect a period of success until he sees another sign that the tide has turned against him, when he must again get out of the market.

I have always made the biggest profits after I have remained out of the market for a long period of time and have always made the biggest losses after I have been in a campaign in the market for a long period of time. No man can trade heavily in the market without having a strain on his nervous system, and when his nerves begin to give way and his health is below normal, his judgment gets bad and he begins to make losses. There is no use staying in, holding on and hoping, when things start going against you. Take your loss quickly and get out.

You will make money by staying out of the market and waiting for an opportunity when the market is right, your physical condition good and your mind at its best. To beat the stock market is a battle of wits. Your mind must be active, keen and alert. You must be able to change your mind and act quickly. When you find that your mind gets sluggish and you cannot act quickly, you are in no position to be in the market. I have been connected with brokerage offices and have known the position of a large number of traders. I have seen the market go against them for days and weeks. Gradually they would start getting out, but a few would be very stubborn and hold on. I call it stubbornness; they called it nerve, but it is not nerve which makes a man hold on when the market is going against him. It is hope and stubbornness. Nerve will not outlast a market that is going against you, and even if the nerve does last, your money will not last to continue to buck the trend. Traders usually talk with each other in the boardroom. When all but two or three have gotten out with losses, they will talk with each other and say they are going to put up more margin, stick it out until the turn comes.

Finally, there is one left, and he will say that he is not going to sell out on the bottom but will see it through. Finally, his hope gives way to despair and he puts in an order to sell at a price on a rally. The market fails to reach his selling price. Then he changes the price for several days and misses it, and the market continues to go lower. Finally, he gives an order to sell out at the market. That was my signal to buy. I would then buy at the market and invariably made profits. This shows that the *trader nearly always does the wrong thing at the wrong* time after he has held on for a long period of time. This proves that the man who has health, money, nerve and knowledge and stays out of the market until the psychological moment can always make big profits.

Some man who has made and lost a lot of money betting on the races wrote the following poem:

"The time to pitch in is when others discouraged show signs of tire. The battle is fought in the home stretch and won twixt the flag and the wire."

It is the ability to act and begin at a time when others see no hope that helps to make a success in speculation. When everything looks the bluest and nobody can see a ray of hope, it is time to buy good stocks. When the pot is boiling and everybody is optimistic, with not a cloud in the sky, it is time to sell. Hope, in one case, has wrecked and ruined judgment and, at the other extreme, fear has caused loss of hope, loss of judgment, and through discouragement, traders sell out on the bottom and many of them go short. This is the wise fool's opportunity and the man who has nerve to wade in at these extremes will make money.

The man with money who is out of the market and is studying and watching his charts can see these opportunities at the extremes and take advantage of them.

FEAR VS. KNOWLEDGE

Fear is one of the great causes of losses in Wall Street. In fact, fear is the cause of most all of our troubles and misfortunes in life. What causes fear? It is ignorance or lack of knowledge. The truth is knowledge whether it is scientific or otherwise, and when a man has knowledge, he sees and knows and does not fear. With knowledge, he does not hope, because he knows what will happen, and does not hope or fear what will happen.

Why does a man sell out stocks at the lowest point? It is because he fears they will go lower. If he knew that they were at the lowest point, he would have no fear, and instead of selling, he would buy. The same applies at the top. Why does a man buy at the highest point or cover shorts at the highest point? Because he has lost hope and fears they are going higher. If he had knowledge, he would have no fear and would use good judgment. To succeed, hope and fear must be eliminated, and the only way to eliminate these two impostors is to get as much knowledge as you can.

WHY TRADERS DO NOT SELL OUT STOCKS AT HIGH LEVELS

In every bull market many traders have enormous profits, but fail to get out at the right time. They let stocks decline and sometimes wipe out 50 to 100 points' profit before selling out. There must be a reason for this. We have heard much talk of Wall Street psychology and some writers have said that the 1929 Wall Street panic was due to mob psychology. This is largely true, but mob psychology would not have caused the panic if previously mob psychology had not caused the big bull market when everybody bought, got over-optimistic and failed to get out with big profits.

The following incident, which actually happened, illustrates why people do not sell out stocks when they have big profits. A gentleman who I have known for many years bought U. S. Steel around 80 in 1921. He held it and received the stock dividend of 40 per cent in 1927. Then, when the new stock declined to 111¼, he bought some when it rallied to 115, and held all of this stock until it advanced to 261¾ in September 1929. Long before the stock crossed 175, he talked about selling it at 200, but when it crossed 200, he decided that it was going to 250, and waited to sell at that price. About the time that U. S. Steel advanced to 250, this man met a friend of mine and said to him, "What does Gann think of Steel now?" My friend replied, "Gann says that the market is going to be top around the end of August and he is going to go short of U. S. Steel." This man said, "I hear that U. S. Steel is going to 300 or higher and then be split up 4 for 1, then I am going to sell out." After U. S. Steel sold at 150 in November 1929, this man came into the office of my friend who said to him "Mr. H., did you sell your U. S. Steel above $250?" He answered, "No, I did not sell it, and I have it yet." My friend said, "Why on earth didn't you sell out when you had such big profits?" The man replied, "Well, you know they have a way of hypnotizing you and putting you to sleep when stocks are up near top, then you don't wake up and realize what has happened until they are down near the bottom and it is too late to sell."

This man's statement shows that people do get hypnotized and do not realize what has happened or what is going to happen until it is too late, which is one of the reasons why they do not sell out stocks at high levels. If investors and traders would only learn to follow up their profits with a stop loss order, which would get them out with a good part of their profits when the decline starts, they would be much better off. What was the use of this man allowing U. S. Steel, which he had bought at the right time, to decline over 100 points and wipe out the biggest part of his profits? Of course, after Steel was down 20 points he did not believe that it would decline 80 or go points more; if he had, he would have sold out. Remember, it is not what you believe, think or hope that counts, but it is what the market does, therefore, you must have some rule to protect your profits, once you have made them. I know of no better automatic protection than the stop loss order.

THE WISE FOOL

The cock-sure trader who thinks he knows it all, follows tips and inside information. He condemns what he does not understand and never makes progress because he thinks he knows it all. Such a man calls a follower of science and charts, a fool, but the follower of charts is a wise fool. The natural or average man considers science as applied to the stock market foolishness and condemns charts because he does not understand how to read them. To him they are foolishness because he does not know the rules by which to read them. He has not had years of experience and has not been trained to properly read or accurately determine the future course of stocks. The successful trader is the man who knows that he does not know it all and who is always trying to learn more. When once a man decides he knows it all about the stock market, he is doomed to failure. When activity decreases, stagnation sets in and when a man no longer continues to learn he goes backward, not forward. A successful man must have a plan and rules and follow them.

CHAPTER IV
TIME CHARTS AND TREND CHANGES

NEW WAY TO READ THE STOCK TAPE

The old way of reading the stock tape was to stand at the ticker and watch for activity to break out in a stock with increasing volume; then buy it or sell it. This theory worked quite well in the days when there were never more than 3 or 4 active leaders at one time. But it will not work now with sometimes as many as 800 different stocks traded in, in one day. There are too many crosscurrents; some stocks are always moving up while others are going down. The man who hangs over the ticker in the broker's office has not been beating the market since 1921, and he will not beat it in the future.

There is a new way of reading the tape. It can be applied to any market in the past and to any market in the future, and it will work provided the man who is trading eliminates the human element and follows cold, mathematical facts, leaving hope and fear out of his judgment. In TRUTH OF THE STOCK TAPE, I said that the proper way to read the stock tape was to stay away from the ticker and analyze stocks after the market has closed. The busy man should get the newspaper after the market closes and note the high and low for the day on the stocks he is interested in. He should glance over the entire list and take notice of the stocks that have a volume of 100,000 shares or more. These stocks are either already leaders or are starting to be leaders. Suppose he has watched a stock for several weeks or months and the sales never reached 10,000 shares in a day; then he picks up the paper some day after the market has closed, and finds that this particular stock has a volume of 25,000 shares. This will indicate that the move is on, up or down, and he should start trading in it. Let this be one of the rules, if a stock has a very large volume of sales in a day and has made a very narrow range in fluctuations, do not buy or sell until it shows a wider range of fluctuations and go with the trend whichever way the move starts. Keep up the daily, weekly, monthly and yearly high and low charts according to the rules and examples given and judge the stock accordingly. This is the new and proper way to read the stock tape.

TIME RECORDS PROVE CAUSE AND EFFECT

By studying past history and knowing that the future is but a repetition of the past, you can determine the cause according to the time and conditions. Sometimes it is necessary to go a long way back to determine the cause, because you must study war, its effect, the conditions before war and what follows. The average man's memory is too short. He only remembers what he wants to remember or what suits his hopes and fears. He depends too much on others and does not think for himself. Therefore, he should keep a record, graph or picture of past market movements to remind him that what has happened in the past can and will happen in the future and should not allow his enthusiasm to get the better of his judgment and buy on hope, thinking that there will never be another panic. Panics will come and bull markets will follow just as long as the world stands and they are just as sure as the ebb and flow of the tides, because it is the nature of man to overdo everything. He goes to the extreme when he gets hopeful and optimistic and again when fear takes hold of him, he goes to the extreme in the other direction.

Traders made the mistake of selling too soon and buying too late in 1929. These mistakes could have been avoided if the traders had kept up charts on individual stocks and on the Averages, because they could have seen that they were making higher bottoms and higher tops all the time, especially those stocks which were in strong position and they should not have sold them short. When the Dow-Jones Averages crossed the high levels of 1919, which was the highest in history, it was a sure indication that the bull campaign was going to last for a long time and that stocks were going very much higher. The buying power of the country had increased. There was more money in the country than ever before. More people had been educated to speculate than ever before in history, and this momentum carried stocks to higher levels than they should have gone on intrinsic value. However, the charts, when properly interpreted, showed the up trend on each different stock right along and the trader would have made no mistake if he had interpreted the charts properly and had followed the trend. Buying and selling on hope or fear is poor business. Every man who makes a trade should make it with a good sound reason and then he must figure that he could be wrong and should place a stop loss order for his protection in case he finds he has made a mistake.

Always look up the stock that you are going to trade in and get its record before you make a trade. If it has had a big move previously or a few years before and seems to be in a narrow, trading range, or what I call a sideways move, leave it alone until it shows some definite move up. If the stock has been a leader in a previous bull campaign or a leader in a previous bear campaign, the chances are that it will not be a leader in the next campaign, unless the chart distinctly shows that it is going to lead in an advance or decline.

Study each stock and each group of stocks and watch how they act on rallies and how they act on reactions, so you can determine whether they are in a section of a bull campaign, which will be resumed later, or whether they are in a bear campaign, which must run out 3 to 4 sections before the bottom is reached. Look over your charts and you will find that each group of stocks and each individual stock when it starts on the down trend runs out 3 to 4 sections. First, it has a sharp decline; then rallies and is distributed; then has another decline; hesitates, rallies and then has another decline; hesitates again and then has a final big break or one we call the clean-out, when investors and everybody get scared and decide that stocks are never going up again and sell out everything. When this final clean-out comes, that is the time to buy for the long pull for another bull campaign.

Profits made over a long period of years can be lost in a decline which will run from 5 to 7 weeks, like the panicky decline from September to November, 1929. Accumulated profits over a long period of time are lost because traders have not protected themselves with stop loss orders. A stop loss order is much better protection for traders because it works automatically. A man may have a mental stop, yet when the price reaches there, he does not sell out. Traders get used to normal markets, which have normal reactions of 10 to 20 points, and they think when the big decline comes and a stock has gone down 10 to 20 points, it has gone low enough and they are not worried. Then the decline continues, as it did in 1929, during the panic, when stocks went down 100 to 200, and 300 points. Then what chance has a trader to get out with his profits or with his capital unless he uses a stop loss order or sells at the market as soon as he sees a decline start.

BEST KIND OF CHARTS TO USE

Traders who condemn charts do not know the right kind of charts to use. They apply the same rules or reasons to all kinds of charts. The charts which fool traders the most are the space charts, either 2, 3, or 5-point moves up and down, because these charts do not take into consideration any time element. The next charts that make the most false moves and fool traders often are the daily high and low charts. The weak point with these daily charts is the fact that they show the minor moves, which are like the ripples in the ocean caused by a pebble. They do not disturb or determine the big move or main trend. Most traders use these kinds of charts.

The best charts to use are the weekly, monthly and yearly charts. The weekly high and low chart is much more valuable than the daily chart because it contains 7 times as much time. The monthly high and low chart is a better guide to the trend than the weekly chart, because it contains over 4 times as much time as the weekly and 30 times as much as the daily chart. The yearly high and low chart is the best guide to the main trend, and if used in connection with the monthly chart, will prove of the greatest benefit to traders and investors. It contains 365 times as much time as the daily chart, 52 times as much as the weekly, and 12 times the amount of the monthly chart, measured by time.

The weekly and daily high and low charts are valuable when the markets are very active and are good to use on very high-priced stocks at the time they are culminating or in the final grand rush, because the daily and weekly will show the first change in trend. They are better to use at the tops of fast moves than they are at the bottom. However, when markets have a quick, sharp, panicky decline, then the daily and weekly charts will help, but the best guides in long pull trading and determining the main trend are the yearly and monthly high and low charts.

TREND ACCORDING TO TIME CHARTS

Charts can show you how a market acts after it has been in a range for 20 days, 20 weeks, 20 months, and 20 years. All of these charts look almost the same as far as space movement is concerned, but why can a big advance take place in a given commodity when the yearly position is the same as the daily? It is because 20 years of time accumulates power and buying influence which can never be accumulated in 20 days, 20 weeks, or 20 months. This is what fools so many chart readers. If a stock is new or a new movement is starting and there is only a few days of accumulation or distribution, then you cannot expect a long campaign one way or the other. Sustained and enduring advances or declines seldom ever occur until sufficient time has elapsed to complete a period of accumulation or distribution. A stock often makes many false starts. It will come back near the bottom several times or will advance near the top several times while distribution is taking place, but when once the accumulating or distributing zone is cleared and the stock breaks out into new territory, then the fast move takes place.

HOW TO STUDY DAILY, WEEKLY, AND MONTHLY CHARTS

Watch the action of the daily moves in the 1st, 2nd, 3rd and 4th stages. If a stock starts up, has an advance, then hesitates and has what we call a sideways movement, and goes on through these Resistance Levels on the up side, then watch how it acts when it hesitates and stops the 2nd, 3rd and

4th times. When it reaches the 3rd or 4th move up, watch for a change in trend as this is the culminating period. You should apply the same rule to the 1st, 2nd and 3rd moves on the weekly and monthly charts. It also applies to the major as well as the minor swings. When a market begins declining or an individual stock starts down, it usually makes 2, 3 and 4 movements before it reaches final bottom. If the trend is going to reverse, it will only make the 1st and 2nd decline and then turn up again. But after a prolonged decline and a 4th move down, you should watch for bottom and change in trend.

DAILY TIME RULE

For daily trading or short swings, a good rule to use is never to buy or sell a stock until it has halted for 2 to 3 days at the bottom or top, which will show you that buying or selling is strong enough to check the advance or decline. Then buy or sell and lace a stop loss order not more than 3 points above or below the extreme high or low point at which the stock halted.

This rule should not be applied in panics. On the days of extreme fluctuations and large volume, it is not necessary to wait 2 or 3 days, because the market will have a sharp, reverse move up or down. Therefore, take profits on the days of a fast advance and, when there are big, panicky declines, cover shorts and wait to see what the market does the following day. For example, March 25, 1929, when the record sales were over 8 million shares and stocks had a wide-open break, you should have covered shorts and waited or bought for a rally. Again on October 24 and 29 and November 13, 1929, which were panic days, there was heavy volume and sharp declines followed by quick rallies.

In slow moving stocks, do not make the mistake of trying to get ahead of the market. Wait until a stock shows that the trend has changed and a move has started. Judge each stock according to its own position and do not expect it to follow the movement of its own group unless its graph shows that it is in position to do so.

If you looked at high and low prices for General Motors from 1921 to 1924, you would note how Chrysler, Hudson Motors and many other motor stocks were advancing while General Motors was very inactive and in a narrow, trading range. Then, when General Motors showed that the main trend had turned up, it continued to advance until 1928 and 1929, when the final top was reached and the main trend turned down.

White Motors, from 1921 to 1925, continued to go down nearly 100 points while General Motors was advancing. Charts on White Motors showed plainly that the trend had turned down, and you should have been selling it short at the same time that you were buying General Motors. This is keeping right on the market and following the trend.

Remember that I put the greatest value on the weekly and monthly high and low charts for determining the change in the major trend. The daily high and low charts make false moves and will often fool you because the change that they show is only of minor importance in many cases.

WEEKLY TIME RULE

One of the best rules to use for the weekly high and low chart is to wait for a reaction of 2 to 3 weeks and then buy. This applies to active stocks, as most of the active stocks will not react more than 3 to 4 weeks before the main trend is resumed. When in a bear market, reverse this rule; sell on rallies of 2 to 3 weeks. Always watch for a change in trend in the 3rd week, up or down.

The weekly rule for rapid advances and rapid declines is to watch for a culmination in the 6th or 7th week, up or down; then buy or sell after watching your daily high and low chart for the week that the stock reaches top or bottom, and place a stop loss order above or below the Resistance Level.

MONTHLY TIME RULE

Stocks that are in strong position and show up trend will seldom ever react into the 2nd month. Your rule should be to buy and place a stop loss order under the previous month's low level. Always watch the point at which advances start, whether from the lowest bottom or 1st, and 3rd, or 4th higher bottoms. These starting points are always buying points with a stop 3 points under. When a stock declines or advances after making top or bottom and the movement runs into the and month, the next important time to watch for a change in trend is the 3rd or 4th month.

All of these rules work best in the stocks that are very active and are fluctuating on large volume of sales. Study your daily, weekly, and monthly high and low charts on the active high-priced stocks and you will learn how well these rules work.

WEEKLY AND MONTHLY TIME CHANGES

The weekly time changes are not as important as the monthly, and these rules apply only to active markets.

Important changes often take place on Monday in the first hour. If a stock opens low on Monday and does not sell lower by 12 o'clock, it is a good sign. Then if it closes strong and higher, it is a better indication for higher prices. The reason Monday is so important is because the public buys or sells heavily in the first hour every Monday and causes higher or lower prices. If the insiders are supporting the market, they take the stocks the public sells and then move the market right on up. If the public is buying and the insiders or pools are not supporting, they fill the public buying orders and then let the market go lower.

The next important day of the week to watch for a change in trend is Wednesday, especially Wednesday afternoon. When a market has been advancing or declining, it often reaches the low level or the high level on Wednesday afternoon or in the first hour Thursday morning.

The next important day of the week is Friday. Traders are suspicious and superstitious, because they play on hope and fear. They fear Friday because it is hangman's day. Most of the old countries hang men on Friday. Traders are afraid of Friday, the 13th, but it often means nothing, all depending on the condition of the market. However, Friday morning is often high or low for the week. The main reason for this is that large traders, who have profits, will close their commitments on Friday and stay out of the market for the short session on Saturday. Another reason is that the Federal Reserve statement, showing brokers' loans, always comes out after the market closes on Thursday. If the market has been weak and declining all week, traders will lose hope and decide to get out Friday and wait, and this often makes the market top Friday, and a decline follows, because short covering has weakened the technical position.

MONTHLY DATES AND CHANGE IN TREND

It is very important to watch how stocks act during the first few days of the month. Important changes often occur between the 1st and 3rd of each month. One reason for this is that customers always receive their statements on the 1st of each month and know just how their accounts stand. They often sell out to secure profits or sell out because their accounts have been weakened by declines. The 10th of the month is also important for a change in trend. The 15th is important but not as much as the 10th. The 20th to 23rd is an important time to watch for a change in trend, as high or low prices are often reached around this time of the month.

My experience has proven that the above dates are important and of value to any trader who will watch them, and will many times help in determining top or bottom.

U. S. Steel Monthly Moves -We have told you before that it is important to watch the dates each month when a stock makes the high and low levels. In this way you will learn more about its movements and will find out whether it makes extreme high or low in the early part of the month, in the middle of the month, or in the latter part of the month. We are giving U. S. Steel as an example, showing you the minor movements as well as the extreme high and low for each month.

1927

January 4th and 5th low; 11th extreme high; 28th extreme low.

February 2nd low; 15th high; 20th low of a reaction; 24th to 28th extreme high for the month.

March 2nd low; 17th to 18th top of rally; 22nd lo w of reaction; 30th and 31st extreme high.

April, first high on the 9th; then low on the 12th and 13th; 18th to 19th top of rally; 22nd low of reaction; 25th and 26th high of rally; then 28th to 30th extreme low.

May 2nd to 3rd low; next high on the 11th; 16th to 17th low of reaction; 21st high of rally; 25th low of next move; 26th extreme high.

June 1st to 2nd extreme high of the month; 14th to 15th low of reaction; 20th top of rally; 30th extreme low.

July 1st to 2nd extreme low; 14th to 15th high of rally; 18th to 19th low of reaction; 29th extreme high.

August 3rd extreme high for the month; 8th to 9th low; then a quick rally on the 10th; 12th low; 30th extreme high.

September 1st and 2nd extreme low; extreme high on the 15th and 16th; low of reaction on the 19th; rallied to the 26th; 29th low of reaction.

October 4th high; low on the 10th; rallied to the 14th and declined to extreme low on the 29th.

November 1st extreme low; 15th top of rally; 17th low of reaction; 19th high of rally; 21st and 22nd low of reaction; 26th and 29th extreme high.

December 1st to 2nd high; then 9th low of reaction; rallied to the 16th and 20th; reacted to the 21st and on the 24th made extreme high; then low again on the 30th.

1928

January 3rd and 4th high of rally; declined to the 10th and 11th; rallied to the 14th; declined to the 18th; then on the 27th made extreme high.

February 4th low; rallied to the 9th; reacted and made low on the 20th; rallied to the 23rd; declined and made extreme low for the month on the 27th.

March 2nd extreme low; 17th top of rally; 24th low of reaction; 26th high of rally; 27th decline; 31st extreme high.

From this time on, as Steel is more active, we will give only the dates for the early part of the month, extreme high and low for the month, and how the stock closes the month.

April 2nd to 3rd low; 12th extreme high for the month; 24th extreme low; 30th closed the month near the extreme low.

May 3rd low; 11th extreme high; 22nd extreme low; 25th top of rally; 29th near the low for the month.

June 1st high for the month; 25th extreme low, rallied to the 29th.

July 2nd low; rallied to the 9th, followed by decline to the 12th and 17th, making extreme low; 28th extreme high; closed 3 points off from the high.

August 3rd and 8th extreme low; 29th extreme high; closed near the top for the month

September 5th extreme low; 22nd high for the month; closed near the top.

October 3rd extreme low; 15th and 24th high; closed 6 points below the top.

November 1st to 3rd extreme low; 16th to 17th extreme high; closed 6 points down from the top.

December 4th extreme high; a big decline followed reaching lows on the 8th and 14th; closed the month 11 points up from the low levels.

1929

January 3rd first high; 8th extreme low; 25th extreme high; declined 13 points to the 30th and closed the month 9 points down from the top.

February 2nd high for the early part of the month; declined 20 points to the 16th, making extreme low; rallied to the 26th and closed 5 points down from the top and up 16 points from the extreme low.

March 1st high for the month; 6th and 11th same low of reaction; 15th top of rally; 26th extreme low; closed 12 points up from the low.

April 12th extreme high; 17th low of reaction; 30th top for the month; 3 points down from the high at the close.

May 1st high for the month; 31st extreme low, the stock selling at 162½, the last low before the big advance started.

June 3rd extreme low; 28th extreme high; closed the month at the top.

July 1st extreme low; 24th extreme high; closed the month 4 points down from the high.

August 1st extreme low; 14th top for a reaction; declined 9 points on the 10th; advanced and made extreme high on the 24th; closed 4 points down from the top.

September 3rd extreme high for the month as well as the highest price in its history, when the stock reached 261½; 13th to 16th low of reaction, down 31 points; 19th top of big rally, up 17 points; 30th extreme low for the month.

October 4th low 206½; 11th high 234; 24th low 193½ on the first panic day; 25th high 207; extreme low on the 29th, the day of the big panic, when the stock sold at 166½; rallied to 193½ on the 31st and closed the month at 193.

November - This month ended the panicky decline and Steel made extreme low on the 13th, reaching 150; rallied to 171¾ on the 21st; declined to 160¾ on the 27th and closed the month at 162.

December 2nd low 159¼; 10th high 189; 23rd low 156¾; closed the month at 166½.

1930

January 2nd extreme low 166; rallied to 173¼ on the 10th; declined to 167¼ and closed the month at 184.

February, made high for the month on the 14th and 18th at 189½; reached extreme low on the 25th at 177.

March 13th extreme low at 177¾; a sharp rally followed and the stock reached 195, the extreme high, on the 31st, closing the month at 194.

April 3rd low 192¾; 7th high 198¾; reacted to 192¼ on the 14th.

Study these minor swings each month and note where the bottoms and tops are made, so that you will know when Resistance Levels are crossed on the up side or broken on the down side. The more you study time and space movements on each individual stock, the more successful you will be in trading in it. Study the volume of sales at each important bottom and top and consider the number of shares outstanding in each stock. This will help you to determine whether buying is better than selling or not.

It is important to study past movement of stocks to see how much time is usually required to complete a movement. There are several sections to a major movement or swing. There are yearly and seasonal changes in all stocks, and you must watch for these seasonal changes. It is also important to watch for change in trend every 3rd, 6th, 9th and 12th month, but the most important time to watch for a major change in trend is at the end of each year. By this, I do not mean the calendar year. For example, if a stock makes bottom in the month of August, and the trend continues up; then the most important date would be the following August or one year later, when you should watch for at least a change in the minor trend, which might last one to 3 months or more.

I have repeatedly stated that stocks, like individuals, have habits and that to determine the position of any stock, you must study it individually and not collectively. The farther back you have a record of a stock and the more you study it, the more you will understand its actions and know when it is making tops and bottoms.

Study Swing Charts of U. S. Steel from 1901-1930. You can see how the important tops and bottoms were formed and where the important changes in trend have taken place in the different years. U. S. Steel has made more tops and bottoms in January and February, and in May and June, and in October and November than in any other months, as the records will show. It has made more bottoms in February than in any other month. Therefore, knowing these months, you can watch for a change in trend either way and it will be a great help to you.

U. S. Steel - 1901 low in May; 1902 high in January; 1903 low in May; 1904 extreme low in May. 1905 low of reaction in May; 1906 February high; 1907 January high; extreme low in October; 1908 high in November; 1909 low in February and extreme high in October. 1910 February low of reaction, November top of rally. 1911 February high, a second high in May and low of the year in November. 1912 February low, and May low of a reaction; October high of the year. 1913 June low, August high, low of a reaction in October. 1914 February high; last top of rally in May. Exchange was closed from July to November 1914, but U. S. Steel made the lowest price on the New Street Curb in November. 1915 extreme low in February. 1916 extreme high in November; 1917 low in February, extreme high for the year in May; 1918 top for a reaction in February, high in May, low of a reaction in June, and high of year in August. 1919 low of the year in February, high of last rally in

43

October; 1920 low in February for a rally; 1921 extreme low of the year in June. 1922 high of the year in October; low of a reaction in November. 1923 October last low, from which a big advance started. 1924 high in February for a reaction; extreme low of the year in May. 1925 high in January for a reaction and high for the year in November. 1926 high in January for a reaction, low of a big reaction in October.

1927- Note that the old stock made high for the year in May and that the new stock made extreme low in January, extreme high in September and low of a big reaction in October. 1928 top in January for a reaction, low of the reaction in February, last low in May, from which the final big advance started. 1929 first high in January, low of a reaction in February, last low in May, from which the big advance started which culminated on September 3, 1929, when the stock reached 261¾, the highest in history. Then followed the big break in October and the extreme low for the year 1929 was reached in November. 1930 low of reaction in early part of January, top of rally February 18; reacted 12 points to February 25th and advanced to 198¾ on April 7, the high up to this writing.

From the above you can see that a man who studied U. S. Steel closely for the first 8 or 10 years of its history from, say, 1901 to 1911, would have learned the fact that it made important changes in trend in January, February, May, June, October and November. The knowledge of this fact, together with a study of his charts, would have helped him in determining when tops and bottoms would be reached.

General Motors - It is important to review and study the history of fluctuations of General Motors from the time it was listed on the New York Stock Exchange in 1911 up to date and in this way you will learn the months when it makes the most tops and bottoms.

1911, August high 52. 1912, January and February low 30; August and September high 42. 1913, low 25 in June. 1914, May high 99; July low 55. 1915, January low 73; December high 567. 1916, April low of reaction 405; October extreme high 850. At this time a stock dividend was declared and trading began in the new stock. 1917, January high on new stock 146, April low 98, July high 127, October extreme low of the year 74¼. 1918, February high 141; March low 113, August high 164; September and October low 111. 1919, November high 400. 1920, February low 225; March high 410, where the stock was split up on the basis of 10 for one. March 1920, high on the new stock 42, equal to 420 on the old stock. 1921, January high 16; August low 9½. 1922, the stock was very dull and narrow, reached extreme low of 8¼ in March. 1923, April and May high 17, another narrow year of fluctuations. 1924, April and May last low 12¾; here the stock was exchanged on a basis of 10 of the old stock for 4 of the new. Activity started in the new stock soon afterwards. 1924, May and June low of 52 on the new stock. 1925, November high 149; reacted in December to 106, only a three weeks' reaction and never broke this point until the stock advanced to new high levels. 1926, August high 225. A stock dividend was declared. 1927, October high 282, when another stock dividend was declared. The new stock sold as low as 111 in August 1927, and made high in October at 141; declined in November and December to 125. 1928, May high 210; June low of reaction 169; October and November high 225. Then there was another stock dividend declared. Trading began in the new stock in December 1928. The high this month was 90 and the low 78. 1929, March high 91¾; July low of reaction 67; September high of last rally 79¾; October extreme low for the year 33½. 1930, up to this writing in April General Motors has advanced to 54.

General Motors, Important Months - From the above and from monthly high and low prices, you can see that General Motors has reached the most important tops and bottoms during the months of

March, April, May, August, September and October. In going over the years consecutively, you can see how the highs and lows predominate in these months. Therefore, if you study General Motors and watch the months that it has made highs and lows, then watch these months again the following years, it will help you to determine the tops and bottoms.

1911, high in August. 1912, high in September. 1913, a narrow market, but low in June. 1914, high in May. 1915, low in January; high in December. 1916, low of a reaction in April; extreme high in October. 1917, high in January; low of a reaction in April; extreme high in October. 1917, high in January; low of a reaction in April; low of the year in October. 1918, low in March; high in August. 1919, high for the year in November. 1920, high on both the old and new stock in March. 1921, low in August, rallied to October. 1922, low in March; made same highs August to October. 1923, high in April and May. 1924, last low in April and May. The new stock made low in May 1924. 1925, high in November; low of reaction in December. 1926, high in August, low in November. 1927, stock dividend declared in August; new stock low in August; high in October; reacted in November and December. 1928, high in May, low of reaction in June, high in October and November. 1929, high in March, low of reaction in July, last high of rally in September, and extreme low of the year in October. This shows you that if you watch the months of March, April, May, August, September and October, you will catch the important turns on General Motors.

CHAPTER V
SUCCESSFUL STOCK SELECTING METHODS

BUYING OUTRIGHT

So many traders get the idea from what they read and from what other people say, that there is only one sure way to beat the stock market, and that is by buying outright. Buying stocks outright has just as many disadvantages as any other method. To buy stocks outright at the right time is wise and will result in profits, but what the investor and trader needs to know is the right time to buy stocks outright. As a rule, when the right time comes it is just as safe to buy them on 25 to 50 per cent margin, as it is to buy them outright, because if they are going up, you buy them at the right time and this amount of margin is ample for your protection and will reduce your interest charges. Many people have lost their entire fortune or a large part of their invested capital simply by thinking they were safe because they held stocks all paid for. They continued to let them decline until dividends were passed or until the stocks went in the hands of a receiver and became worthless. Now, if they had bought these stocks on margin, or bought them outright protected with a stop loss order in case the trend should change, they would have saved themselves enormous losses.

The only time that I consider it 100 per cent safe to buy stocks outright and hold them is to buy stocks that are selling below $12 a share and then only risk about 10 per cent of your capital on this class of stocks, because they can go down to nothing and be assessed. Going back over records we find that a large percentage of stocks which have reached very high levels and become seasoned dividend-payers, have almost all at some time in their history sold below $10 per share and some of them sold as low as $3 or $4 per share, so the man that buys them outright when they are selling below 12, certainly cannot lose more than $12 per share. If he buys them at any other higher level and does not protect with a stop loss order, he can lose all he paid for them, or at least a large per cent of his capital. There comes a time in the history of nearly every good stock when you can buy it at a very low level; then later there comes a time when it reaches extreme high levels, where it should be sold. When stocks reach extreme high levels, some of them never reach them the second time and others require 20 to 30 years to get back to these extremes.

NORMAL OR AVERAGE MOVES

You should study the daily average moves, the weekly average moves, and the monthly average moves on each individual stock that you are trading in or intend to trade in. It is important to know the normal average and the abnormal average. Abnormal moves do not come close together and do not last very long. Suppose you were trading in U. S. Steel. You should have its entire history and know what was the greatest move it made between high and low in any month or in any week or in any day. Go back for a year or two from where you intend to start trading and get its average moves for the days, weeks and months, so that you will know when it breaks into activity and starts into an abnormal move, up or down, study the volume of sales at the culmination of moves, either at tops or bottoms. Many traders make a success trading in a stock while it is making normal swings, and then just as soon as it goes into an abnormal swing they start losing money. Remember that you can always get into the market wrong and the way to protect yourself and keep from getting out wrong is to use a stop loss order. It is financial suicide to get into the market wrong and then get out wrong; in other words, to hold on to a loss until it runs into an enormous loss, when you could have taken a quick small loss.

HIGHER BOTTOMS AND LOWER TOPS

You should always watch the bottoms and tops for a sign of a change in trend. Do not be in a hurry. Wait until the other fellow blazes the trail and shows you that the market has turned. If you are waiting to sell short, it is always safer to sell after a stock has made one or two lower tops and lower bottoms, which will show you that the trend has reversed. The same rule applies when you are waiting to buy a stock. You should watch it until it begins to raise the bottoms and the tops. If a stock cannot make a higher bottom and hold it for a few days, or a week, it certainly is in a weak position and should not be bought. At times, a stock will make a higher bottom but fail to make a higher top, that is, not cross the level from which the last decline started. This indicates that the buying power is not strong enough to overcome the selling which started the previous decline. What you want to do is go with the trend, not against it. It pays in the long run to wait until you have a definite indication before making your commitments.

An important sign for you to watch for a top or bottom is a series of days of narrow fluctuations with small volume. If a stock advances sharply on large volume; then has a quick decline, rallies, on a smaller volume, fails to get back to its extreme high level, and remains for several days near the top of the rally in a narrow range with small volume, it means that the buying power is not there and that the stock is unable to advance. You should either go short after a few days of dullness or sell short just as soon as the stock breaks under the level of days of narrow fluctuations and small volume. Then place a stop loss order just above the extreme high levels.

This same rule can be applied at the bottom. After a panicky decline on large volume, if a quick rally follows, it means that shorts are covering; then if the stock reacts, gets back near the extreme low level, but does not break it and the fluctuations narrow down and the volume gets smaller, it is an indication that the selling has subsided and that there is not enough selling pressure to force prices lower. You should either buy and place a stop loss order under the extreme level or just as soon as the stock crosses the level of narrow fluctuation days, then buy, as it will indicate that the trend is turning up.

POPULAR TRADING PRICES

The human mind works in the same way most of the time. People get used to certain figures and they trade at these prices more than any others. The average man thinks in multiples of fives and tens. The popular trading prices are 25, 40, 50, 60, 75, 100, 150, 175, 200, 210, 225, 240, 250, 275, 300, 325, 350, 375 and 400. The public nearly always has these figures in mind as buying or selling points, and that is why a stock will often fail to reach these points either up or down. Therefore, you should watch the action of a stock and when it gets within a few points of these even figures, buy or sell before they are reached.

For example, if everybody has orders in to sell a stock at 50, it may advance to 48 or 49 or even make 49½ and not go any higher. The wise man will watch his chart and see how it acts around these even

48

figures and sell out in time and not try to get the price that everybody else is missing. Often, when a stock is selling above 100, traders will place large orders to buy when it declines to 100. The stock will decline to 102 or even 100 and fail to make 100. The wise man does not try to get the last eighth but buys when it gets near the price and when his chart shows a support level. Many traders buy around 100 with a close stop and calculate that the stock should not break an even figure or 100. The insiders know this and know that the stops are in; therefore they break the stock quickly to around 98, 97 or 96, catching stop loss orders. This gets the traders discouraged; then the stock goes right on up. As a general rule, a stock that is in a strong position and once gets much above 100 does not again decline to 95.

If you are waiting to buy stocks around these figures, you should always buy them when they go through. If I wanted to buy a stock above 200, I would expect it to make about 202 or 203; then possibly break back 7 to 10 points; then come up again two or three times to around 202 or 203. I would watch it about the third time that it went through the even figure or 200 and if the volume was large, I would buy it, expecting a quick run to 210, possibly 225. If it went through 210 easy, I would look for 225, which is always a strong resistance point. It might go a little over this figure or it might not quite reach it and then react to around 215, but when the stock crossed 225 after the second or third attempt, I would buy it for 240, possibly 250.

The same applies to a stock when it reaches 300. It will meet a lot of short selling around the even figure, but when once it goes through after making several attempts, it will move up fast to 325, 350, or 375. I consider that the resistance would be stronger around 355 to 360 than at any other point after it crosses 300. When a stock reaches 400, it is no longer in the class of the small traders and is generally split up and distributed to the public. Stocks are put up to sell. Every man who owns a share of stock expects to sell it some day and will sell it when it reaches a price at which he thinks it is too high.

The public does most of its trading in stocks selling between 50 and 100. Professional traders prefer to trade in stocks selling between 100 and 200. They know that the big money is made in stocks from 150 up to 300. When stocks are split up and stock dividends declared, in most cases they are divided up so that the price of the new stock will sell between 25 and 75, because the insiders know that these are favorite prices for the public to buy.

Knowing all this, your rules should be to trade in the active, fast movers, use stop loss orders, and you will make the most money.

WHY STOCKS MOVE FASTER AT HIGH LEVELS

You can make money faster trading in stocks selling above 100 than you can in stocks selling around 50, and stocks selling above 200 or 300 move faster and make wider ranges than stocks selling around 100, because when stocks reach these levels, there is a reason for it, and the general public seldom trades in stocks selling above 200. When they are in this territory, they are in the hands of millionaires and multimillionaires, who buy and sell on a large scale and cause wide ranges in prices in a short length of time. Therefore, it always pays to trade in active, high-priced stocks. You will make the most money trading in stocks selling above 100 per share and can make the quickest money trading in stocks selling above 200. Stocks selling below 50 make more false moves and have more reactions than stocks selling at higher levels, because they either are in the hands of the public or have not yet sold high enough to establish public confidence and buying power enough to sustain rapid moves.

There are two stages when stocks move fast. One is when the company is very young and the stock is first distributed. The underwriters or promoters support the stock and rush it up fast to attract public attention, and, after distribution is completed, they withdraw support, and as the public is holding the bag, the stock declines.

Stocks also have fast moves after the companies are many years old and have established a record of good earnings and have paid dividends for a long period of time. Investors gradually absorb these stocks and the floating supply becomes smaller. The investors hold when the stock advances and do not sell out. Therefore, it is easy for manipulators to move the stock up fast, because they do not have to buy large amounts of stocks on the way up.

OLD TOPS AND OLD BOTTOMS

The great value of having charts going back ten years or more - if the stock is that old - is to enable you to know where the previous tops and bottoms have been made and when the stock has crossed these old levels. This has been fully covered in TRUTH OF THE STOCK TAPE, but I want to give you some rules that will help you.

Suppose a stock has made a top around 100 for several months previous or several years previous. When it crosses 100, we have every reason to believe that it is going higher to 110, 125 or possibly 150, and you should buy it. Then it advances to 103. Now, if the stock is going higher in the near future, it should not react to 97 after it sells at 103. Therefore, your stop should be at 97. If it reacts this far, it may mean that the main trend has changed but it will indicate that, in all probabilities, it is not going to advance in the immediate future and you had better be out of it.

FIRST ADVANCE AND FIRST DECLINE

It is very important to watch the first reaction after an advance gets under way. In many stocks, this will amount to about 5 to 7 points. In more active, high-priced stocks, it will run 10 to 12 points, but whatever the reaction is, watch it and expect about the same reactions from different levels. For example, U. S. Steel from 1907 to 1909 and 1914 to 1919. If you had bought after a reaction of 5 to 7 points from any high level, you would always have made money, but if you had bought after the stock reacted 10 points, it was a danger signal, and you should have sold out on the next rally. Stocks always have reactions on the way up. These are simply resting periods. They must also have rallies on the way down. These rallies are the result of short covering and buying by people who believe the stock has gone low enough. You must realize the importance of buying and selling in time and not wait until the last hour to act. It is better to get out too soon than too late. Watch for the second or third top or bottom and if the stock fails to go as high or as low as the first top or bottom, then get out and wait.

HOW TO BALANCE A STOCK

You can use the ledger system and balance a stock just the same as you can balance your books. Your ledger will show you when your stock is closing with gains or losses. If it continues to close with a loss or close lower, the trend is down, and there is no reason to buy until it shows something on the credit side. You must watch the days, weeks and months when a stock closes higher or lower. It is very important when a stock closes near the same level for three or more days. When it closes higher or lower than this level, it is an indication that it is going to move in that direction, especially if the market is very active and the volume of trading increases the day that the stock closes higher or lower. Always watch your volume, because it shows whether the energy or power, which moves the market, is increasing or decreasing.

THE RULE OF THREE

This is one of my discoveries of a method for making big profits in a short time trading in active, fast-moving stocks. I have made a lot of money with it and some traders have paid me as much as $1,000 for this method. I am now giving you the benefit of it in this book. The rule is this: A stock which shows strong up trend will never close 3 consecutive days with losses. When it does close 3 consecutive days with losses, then it indicates that the trend has reversed, at least temporarily, and the longer a stock runs before making 3 days' reactions, or closing 3 days at lower prices than the previous days, the surer indication it will be that the move is over. The same rule applies when a stock is declining. It will never close more than 2 days with gains or at higher prices. When it does close for 3 consecutive days with a gain, or a balance on the credit side, then it indicates that the trend has reversed, at least temporarily, and may mean a big move up. It makes no difference how high or low a stock goes during the market hours; the price at which it closes shows whether it has made a gain or loss over the previous day and whether it should be placed on the credit or debit side of your ledger. This is one of the most valuable rules for trading in high-priced active stocks. It will help you to get the benefit of the fast advances or declines and enable you to know when the minor trend is changing. Apply this same rule to the weekly and monthly high and low charts.

VOLUME OF SALES

In comparing the total volume of sales on the New York Stock Exchange from 1921 to 1929 with the record of former years, we must take into consideration the increase of stocks listed on the Exchange and the increase in shares caused by stock dividends, split-ups and new corporations formed. While this was very large during these years, at the same time the increase in the volume of sales with stocks at the highest prices in history, means that distribution has been the greatest of any time in history and that the reaction or decline which must follow will be in proportion to the volume of sales and the heights to which stocks have risen.

The volume of trading is just the same as a large volume of water. If it is two or three times greater than normal, it must spread over a larger area, break the dams and do great damage. When the flood gates of Wall Street are open and the millions of speculators and investors start to liquidate, all former records will be broken, the avalanche of selling will carry prices lower than the most sanguine pessimist ever dared to imagine. (The above was written on August 4, 1929, when Mr. Gann began writing the "Wall Street Stock Selector.")

The volume of sales always increases when stocks advance. This applies to days, weeks, months and years. When liquidation is going on and has about run its course, the volume decreases. The years of bear markets always show small volume and the years of bull markets always show very large volume.

It is important to study the yearly volume of sales on the New York Stock Exchange. Examining the total sales of stocks traded in on the New York Stock Exchange from 1875 to 1929 will show you that in 1875 to 1878, yearly sales were only 40 to 50 million shares. The last year sales dropped to as low as 40 million shares was in 1878. In 1882, when the bull market culminated, sales reached 120 million shares. In 1894 and in 1896, the bottom of a prolonged bear market, sales again dropped to 50 million shares for the year. Then followed the McKinley boom, with the volume of sales getting larger every year until 1901, when sales reached 266 million. From the top of this bull campaign, sales decreased on the reaction or bear market which followed, as they always do in a bear market, getting down to 160 million in 1903. In the bull campaign which culminated in 1906, total sales broke all records again, reaching 284 million. After that the volume of sales was smaller every year until 1914 when they reached 48 million, the lowest since 1896. But the fact must not be overlooked that the Exchange was closed for over four months at the beginning of the World War. This again shows that when a market is working lower, the volume of sales is very small in the last year of a bear campaign, which shows that liquidation has run its course. After 1914, sales increased and in 1919 broke all records, reaching 310 million shares. In the bear campaign, which culminated in December 1921, they dropped to 171 million. After that sales increased every year on a greater scale than ever before until 1929, when sales were the largest in history, 1,124,000,000 shares, compared with 171,000,000 in 1921 when the bear market culminated.

During the week ending November 2, 1929 the total volume of sales was 43½ million shares, almost as much as the total volume for the entire year of 1914. Such an enormous volume of sales as this in one year, especially when we consider that the sales for 1928 were 925 million shares, approaching the billion share mark, means that the public bought stocks on a larger scale than ever before and that somebody supplied these two billion shares of stocks in the last two years of the bull market. The total volume of sales during September, October and November, 1929, was 303,230 shares, just a little over one-fourth of the total sales for the year 1929. While there was heavy liquidation and big declines in the panic, this volume of sales does not overbalance the enormous volume of trading for the two years past. It indicates that many stocks will be in a bear market for several years to come and that the volume of sales will be very much smaller before the bear market ends and the next bull market starts. A study of the volume for each week, month, and year on the individual stocks will help you in determining the trend.

U. S. STEEL VOLUME

It is always important to watch the volume of sales daily, weekly and monthly and consider the total shares outstanding of the stock that you are watching. When U. S. Steel sold at 162½ on May 31, 1929, it was down 30 points from the top of March 1, 1929. When it was selling around the top at 192 to 193, the volume of sales daily was running from 125,000 to 250,000 shares. When it reached the low of 162½, the daily volume of sales was running 25,000 or 75,000 shares, showing that the selling pressure was not heavy and that the stock was being accumulated. When Steel crossed 180 on June 21, 1929, note how the volume of sales increased to over 100,000 shares or more daily.

Then on July 8, when it crossed 193, getting into new high territory, sales were 194,000 shares and the volume continued large until July 31, when sales reached 208,000 and the stock closed at 209½, the highest closing price up to that time. August 8, sales 295,000; August 9, sales 263,000; August 12, sales 337,000; August 13, sales 488,700, which was the biggest volume of sales of any day in the year; August 14, sales 296,000. Note that for August 12, 13, and 14, the total sales for the 3 days were 1,121,800 shares, with the price up to 245, advancing in 3 days from 219 to 245 or a gain of 26 points. Notice that from August 19 to 24, the day when the first top was reached at 260½, the sales during these 6 days were 814,200 shares, with the stock up from 238 to 260½, or a gain of 22½ points, on 814,200 shares. From this top a decline followed, which showed a reversal in trend. Note the volume of sales from August 26 to 29, four days, were 247,400 shares, down 9 points. This volume of sales was not yet heavy enough to show that the big move was under way, but it was enough in view of the fact that the stock had closed 4 consecutive days with a loss, which indicated that it would be a short sale on a rally. It only rallied 2 days before the trend turned down again. On August 30 and September 3, the stock advanced 10 points to 261¾. The volume of sales for these two days was 240,200 shares, less on the rally than it was on the decline, showing that the buying power was running out and that the insiders were selling and that the public was buying. The last rush up to August 24 was no doubt short covering in large volume and the public bought. Then when the second rush up came, shorts covered again but not so much and the public bought but not so heavily because they were already loaded up.

From September 3, 1929, note how the volume increased each day on the down side. From September 19, the top of the last rally, to October 4, the total sales were 2,105,800 shares. Note September 19 high 247½, October 4 low 206½, down 41½ points. With sales of over two million shares, it showed that there was heavy liquidation and that the main trend was down. From October 4 a 6-day rally followed, from October 5 to 11. The stock went up from 206½ to 234, an advance of 27½ points from the low, on sales of 846,500 shares. The volume, while fairly heavy, was not enough to overbalance the selling pressure and no doubt most of it was short covering and public buying. People thought the stock was cheap enough after it was down 50 points and bought it, making a mistake. After the trend turned down again on October 11, Steel continued under heavy liquidation until October 29, the stock declining from 234 to 166½, making a decline of 67½ points on total sales of 2,776,100 shares. Note the volume on October 23 and 24 was 668,000 shares for the 2 days, and again on the panic days, October 28 and 29, total sales 592,000 shares. This indicated heavy selling, but liquidation had not run its course. A 2-day rally followed, October 29 to October 31, and Steel advanced 27 points. The volume in these two days was 204,400 shares. This volume was too small to hold the stock up. It indicated only short covering and a small amount of buying, but the manipulators were running the stock up fast to fill these orders. From October 31 to November 13 Steel declined from 193½ to 150, down 43½ points; sales 732,400 shares. This volume indicated that liquidation had run its course, being a smaller number of shares than at the time when Steel sold down to 166½. After November 13 the volume was smaller, sometimes falling below 50,000 shares per day. This was an indication that liquidation was over and that the insiders were only buying the stock when it was offered but not bidding for it. From December 6 to 9, U. S. Steel went up 29½ points on sales of 599,600 shares. This was short covering. Note that on December 9, the day the stock reached top, the sales were 355,500 shares and it closed down 9 points from the top. If this had been good buying Steel would have closed with a gain on the day and near the top, especially with such heavy volume of sales. From December 9 to December 23, Steel declined from 189 to 156¾, down 32¼ points, on sales of 1,260,000 shares. This indicated the last wave of liquidation, probably by people who got scared because they had held on too long after the first rally came, then decided that Steel was going below 150, so they sold out on this second wave. But Steel made a higher bottom, indicating that the stock was well bought and that support was forthcoming on the decline. On December 23, when Steel reached 156 ¾, the total sales for the day were only 111,800 shares, and on November 13, 1929, the day that extreme bottom was reached, the sales were only 97,500 shares. These small volumes of sales at the extreme low of a big decline indicated that liquidation had run out and that there was not much more stock for sale.

It is important to add up the total volume of sales that a stock makes in going from an extreme low to an extreme high. On December 22, 1928, the low on U. S. Steel was 149¾ and it worked higher all the time from this level until September 3, 1929, when it reached 261¾. The total sales during this period were 18,895,000 shares. The total outstanding shares of U. S. Steel are only a little over 8 million. Thus, in this advance the total outstanding shares changed hands twice. From May 31, 1929, when the stock sold at 162½ the last time, being down 30 points from the high of March, it advanced to 261¾ on September 3, 1929, being up nearly 100 points. The total sales during this period were 7,615,100 shares, almost as much as the entire capital stock outstanding. Then, during the period from September 3, 1929, when the stock made top at 261¾, to November 13, 1929, when it reached a low of 150, the total sales were 7,365,300 shares. Note how near these two total volumes of sales came being equal. This was another good indication for bottom, when the number of shares on the decline equaled or nearly equaled the number of shares on the advance. However, when we consider the total number of shares traded in from 149¾ to 261¾ and then back to 150, there is a vast difference because the comparison of 18,895,000 shares against and 7,365,300 on the decline, covering the same number of points, indicated manipulation on the way up and that there must have been a large number of wash sales in order to attract the public and get them to buy stock. There are always less wash sales on a decline than there are on an advance. Actual sales and real liquidation take place on declines while a lot of stock is bought and washed on the way up. It requires heavy buying to attract attention in putting stocks up, but when liquidation gets under way it is not necessary to do anything but just let the public sell and get out.

If you will study the daily, weekly and monthly volume of sales on culminations of each different stock, you will find it very helpful in judging when it is in a strong or weak position.

WHEN A STOCK IS IN EXTREMELY WEAK OR STRONG POSITION

I have often said that a stock was in such a strong position that it could not react. This occurs when a stock has advanced and crossed high levels made many years previous. Then, investors who have carried the stock for years, sell out. People who know that the stock is going higher, buy it all at high levels and the floating supply becomes scarce; then a fast runaway move takes place. For example, American Can crossing 68 in 1925, the highest in history up to that time, continued to advance with very little reactions. American Smelting made a high of 174½ in 1906; then, in 1925, when it crossed this level, the investors all sold out and the professional traders went short. The stock was in such a strong technical position that it could not react and advanced another 100 points. When a stock is in this position, you should never sell it short. It is safer to buy than it was at lower levels. It takes nerve to buy stocks at extreme high levels but nerve is what helps you to make money. Certainly somebody

54

knew that American Smelting was worth more money than 175, or they would not have bought all of the stock at such a high level. The fact that such a long period of time had elapsed from the time it sold there before showed that there was some good reason for it to go still higher.

A stock gets into an extremely weak position, where it cannot rally, except very small rallies, after it has had a prolonged advance. Traders and investors gain confidence in the stock and buy it on every little reaction, until finally the stock is well distributed and overbought. Then, when a decline starts, there are no buying or supporting orders on the way down and when investors and traders, who have bought at higher levels, start selling out, the stock gets weaker all the time and rallies get smaller

For example: Foundation Company had a big advance in 1925, made top at 183¾ in November. There was a big period of distribution. After it broke out of the zone of distribution, it started down and worked lower while other stocks were advancing. After it had been declining for a long time, and investors and traders had been holding on and hoping for a rally, some of them buying on the way down, it finally broke 75 and everybody started to sell because they had lost hope. Then, after being down over 100 points, the stock was in such a weak position that it could not rally. It was a safe short sale at this level and profits could have been made just as quickly as if you had sold it short around 180. It declined to 13 in November 1929.

Another stock which got into such a weak position that it could not rally was Advance Rumely after the pool collapsed. International Combustion Engineering was another stock that was overbought and after it had declined 50 points was in such a weak technical position that the rallies were much smaller than when it was 50 points higher.

Don't be afraid to sell stocks after they have had big declines because they are in a weaker position and safer short sales than when they are at higher levels.

DETERMINING RIGHT TIME TO SELL

Many traders get into a stock right, but get out wrong. They may have bought right, but they do not know when to sell, or what rules to follow to determine when the stock has reached top. Suppose you get in a stock after it has gone through a long period of accumulation, such as U. S. Cast Iron Pipe, Crucible Steel, and Wright Aero. You want to get the maximum profits once you get in right and there are certain signs that you must watch in order to know when it is time to sell. Stocks in the early stages of a bull market always creep, or move up slowly, having many reactions, but when they come to the finish or final grand rush and reach the boiling point, there is a fast move up. Your rule should be: Wait to sell your stock until it boils, so long as it is moving in your favor and you can follow it up with a stop loss order. Most stocks that are very active finish a bull campaign with a fast advance, lasting 6 to 7 weeks, sometimes as much as 10 weeks, moving very fast. At these times the volume is usually extra large, which indicates that there is big buying and selling going on and that the stock is being advertised for distribution purposes. As a rule, a fast advance of 6 to 7 weeks marks the culmination of an upward swing, just as a fast decline of 6 to 7 weeks especially on heavy volume, when there is a panicky decline, marks the end of a bear campaign, when you should cover shorts and wait.

For example: On May 31, 1929, the last low on U. S. Steel was 162½. A big move started and at no time did the stock react more than 7 points until August 14, when it reached a high of 245, up 82½ points. It reacted to 235, down 9 points, the first sign of the end of the upward rush, after over 10 weeks' fast move up. However, it did not close 3 days lower at any time until it sold at 261¾ on September 3, up nearly 100 points in 3 months. One of our rules is that when a stock has advanced 85 to 100 points in a short time, or declined this much, you should watch for top or bottom and get out. If a trader had been following U. S. Steel up all the way from the bottom with a stop 10 points away, his stop loss order would never have been caught until after Steel sold at 261¾; then if he got out and went short on a break of 10 points, he could have followed down and made big profits. Steel had a fast move down from September 3, just the same as it had a fast move up, declining 111 points on heavy volume from September 3 to November 13, a period of less than 12 weeks. From the last rally point, October 11 to November 13, Steel declined from 234 to 150, a decline of 84 points in less than 5 weeks, which would have been a warning to cover shorts and wait or buy for another rally, knowing that these fast, panicky declines cannot last any more than the final grand rush on the up side can last. They always mark the end of a campaign one way or the other.

Vanadium Steel is another example of one of these fast moves up. The last low on Vanadium was 65½ on February 25, 1930; advanced to 124½ on March 25, up 59 points in 4 weeks and up 87 points from November 13, 1929, low. Making top on heavy volume indicated a reaction to follow, especially after being up 87 points in so short a time. It was moving up too fast and the last advance was the result of short covering. Vanadium reacted quickly to 104, down over 20 points in a few days. Remember that sharp reactions follow from tops where there is a final grand rush after a fast move up and the same way in most cases where a stock is very active after a fast move down. The first rally is very swift and runs a considerable number of points before a secondary reaction and a settling period takes place. Therefore, watch for these fast moves both up and down to sell out long stocks and cover shorts, but remember don't buck the trend, place a stop loss order, or get out quickly if a stock starts moving against you. These fast moves up and down, which many stocks have, show how silly it is for a trader to buy or sell against the trend and expect to put up margin and hold on. These fast moves are the moves to pyramid on and not to be bucked and held on against the trend.

SIDEWAYS MOVEMENTS

You often hear traders say: A stock can only go two ways, up or down, and that it should be easy to keep right on the market. This statement is not exactly correct. If stocks always moved straight up or straight down, it would be easy to make money, but stocks often have sideways moves. While they are in a movement of this kind, they hold in a narrow, trading range sometimes weeks or months, getting neither higher nor lower than a previous top or bottom. Moves of this kind fool traders many times and cause losses. A stock starts up and they think it is going higher, but stops, reacts, gets back around the old bottom, and they think it is going lower and sell it short, but it stops and goes up again. When a stock is in a position of this kind, the only thing to do is to leave it alone until it breaks out of an area one way or the other. After it gets out of the sideways movement, which is always accumulation or distribution, and breaks into new high or new low territory, then you can trade in it with some certainty of having determined the correct trend.

Jewel Tea - This is a good example of a sideways movement. The advance started in January 1922, and reached top at 22 in May 1922: declined to 14 in August 1922; advanced to 24 in February, 1923, failing to get 2 points above the high of May 1922; declined to 15¾ in October 1923; advanced to 23 in January 1924; declined to 16½ in April; advanced to 22½ in August and December 1924; declined to 15¾ in July, August, and September 1925. Then finally in December 1925, the advance started and it crossed all the highs from 1922 to 1925. From a chart you can see that the stock was in a sideways movement during 1922, 1923, 1924, and 1925. It never broke under the low of August 1922, and never advanced 3 points above the high of May 1922, during these 4 years. The narrow fluctuations over this period would have fooled traders many times, but the trader who waited for the stock to break the low made in August 1922, or advance 3 points above the high of May 1922, made money when he did make a trade and made it quickly because he would not have bought or sold it before the big move started. When the stock did cross these levels and showed which way it was going to move, the trend continued up without a change until it advanced to 179 in November 1928.

Leave stocks alone when they are in a sideways movement and always use the rule of waiting until they cross 3 points above the old top level or break 3 points under the old low level before making your commitments. Following this rule will save you many months and weeks of waiting and prevent losses, because if you wait until the stock gets into new territory before you get in, you certainly will have a better chance to place a close stop loss order, which will protect you or get you out in case the stock is not going to move, while if you make a trade when it is in a sideways movement between two points, your chances for making profits are much smaller. These sideways moves are periods of rest and preparation for a new move one way or the other way.

BUYING AND SELLING AT EVEN FIGURES

The human mind follows the trend of the least resistance. From the time of primitive man, we have learned to count, figure, and buy and sell. Traders often make the mistake of placing buying or selling orders at even figures. A stock will sometimes advance to within ¼ or ⅛ of an even figure and go near it several times and never make it.

Why? Because there is so much selling at the even figure that the pools or insiders will not take the stock before it has a reaction which will shake out people who are waiting to get out at an even figure. It is the same about buying. Traders see a stock selling around 55 or 56 and put an order in to buy on a reaction at 50. The stock declines to 51, 50¼, or 50⅛ and they fail to get their orders executed because there were so many buying orders at 50 and the demand was so good that the insiders, knowing these orders were there, would not sell the stock at 50, but supported it just above this level.

Even figures not only apply to 25, 30, 35, 40, 45, 50, 55, 60, 65, 70, 75, 80, 85, 90, 95, 100, etc., but to even figures at other prices, as 58, 62, 73, 86, etc. Put your buying and selling order ⅛ or ¼ below or above the even figure that you decide to trade at. If you want to buy at 62 and the stock is close to that price, put your order at 62¼. If you want to sell at 62, put your order at 61⅞, or if you see the stock hesitating around this price, sell at the market. I never believe in limiting orders. Put the order at the market when it reaches near your figure to buy or sell. You will save money by doing so.

U. S. Steel Trading Levels - A review of U. S. Steel from November 16, 1928, to November 13, 1929, will show you something about Resistance Levels and how the stock is influenced by buying and selling orders at even figures or at certain points.

On November 16, 1928, U. S. Steel, high 172½ . There was a quick reaction from the top and another rally. On December 8, 1928, the stock advanced to 172¼. Evidently there were a lot of selling orders around 173, the even figure, and both times the stock stopped at 172½ and 172¼. The traders who had selling orders in at the even figure could not get out and a sharp decline followed. On December 17, 1928, the stock sold at 149¾. In a case of this kind, no doubt traders had stop loss orders in at 150. These orders were caught at the even figure and the stock sold at 149¾ and that was the end of the decline.

Probably other traders, when they saw U. S. Steel break to 149¾, placed buying orders at 149 or 148, and failed to get the stock. Traders who wanted to buy around 150 should have placed their orders at 150¼ or 150⅛; then they would have been sure of having their orders executed. A fast rally followed from this bottom and on January 25, 1929, Steel reached a high of 192¾. This shows you that when it crossed the high levels at 172½ and 172¼, it went right on up 20 points higher. Traders who placed orders the next time to sell at the even figures, 173 and 174, had them executed promptly and were wrong because the stock went higher when it finally did reach these even figures. After selling at 192¾, a sharp decline followed, and on February 16, 1929, the stock reached 168¼. The market was very active at this time and a rally followed and on March 1, it advanced to 193¾, getting just one point above the high of January 25, both times missing the even figure by ¼ point. In the panicky decline which culminated on March 26, 1929, Steel declined to 171½ . Notice that this was around the top of November and December, 1928. Another rally followed and it made top on April 12 at 191⅞. This was the third top. The first top was 192¾, the next at 193¾ and the third at 191⅞.

You might ask why Steel stopped at this level so many times. My answer would be that there was a lot of stock to sell around 194, 195 and on up to 200. The insiders knew this and they would not take the stock at this time. It got up just close enough to the selling orders to make traders hold on; then when a big decline followed, traders who tried to get out at these figures became disgusted and sold out on the decline. On May 31 Steel declined to 162½ . Notice that it broke the lows of February 16 and March 26, 1929, and naturally, traders would get scared and sell out. Stop loss orders were no doubt caught on this decline, because it was 30 points down from the top. From this low level the last final grand rush in Steel started. On July 5, 1929, it sold at 200. Notice that this time, it went right on through the tops at 191⅞ to 193¾. So all the people who had orders in to sell from 195 up to 200 were able to get out. However, the stock stopped exactly on the even figure, 200, and only reacted on July 11 to 197½; then advanced on July 13 to 204, showing that somebody was taking all the stock offered at 200 or above. There is always a lot of stock sold at these round figures and many people go short at prices like 100, 200, 300, etc. On July 16 there was another reaction to 198. Notice that this bottom was ½ point above the level of July 11. This indicates that if people had orders in to buy Steel at 197½, 197, or just around the last bottom, they were not able to buy it. After Steel crossed 200 and advanced to 204, it indicated that it was going very much higher because somebody was taking stock at the highest level in history and there was a large volume of trading. From 198, the last straight, fast move up took place; reactions were very small and on August 24 Steel reached a high of 260½; had a quick reaction on August 29 to 251½ and a final move up to September 3, when the highest price in history was reached at 261¾, getting only 1¼ points higher than the top of August 24. No doubt there were orders in to sell Steel at 262 and on up. That is why it stopped at 261¾. A fast decline followed and on November 7, Steel reached a low of 161½. Notice that this was one point under the low of May 31. Probably traders had stop loss orders in at 162, which were caught, and forced the price one point lower than the previous low level. Then there was a quick rally and on November 8 Steel advanced to 175¾. Then followed the final decline and heavy liquidation, which culminated on November 13, when Steel sold at 150. This time it stopped exactly on an even figure. Notice that the low on December 17, 1928, was 149¾. It is always important to watch these old Resistance Levels or the places where important moves start, as the stock will often be supported the first time and sometimes several times around these old levels. Again the man who wanted to buy Steel around 150 should have placed his order at 150¼ and it would have been executed.

My rule is to place a stop loss order 3 points under these old levels, but it is well to always place it or above or below the even figures.

SELLING STOCKS SHORT AT LOW LEVELS

Many traders think that it is dangerous to sell stocks short that are selling at 75, 50 or 25. It is never dangerous to sell a stock short so long as the trend is down. I will give you an example.

International Combustion Engineering - The high on this stock in February 1929, was 103. It had a sharp decline in March and reached 61 and in May rallied to 80. Now, suppose the trader, when it was selling at 80, had said that it was too low to sell short because it had been as high as 103. In the latter part of May it declined to 56 and in July rallied to 76, failing by 4 points to get back as high as it was in May. When it rallied to around this level it was a cinch to sell it short with a stop above the high level reached in May. It began declining and when it reached 50, breaking under the low level of May, it was again a good short sale, and again a good short sale at 25 or any other place on the way down. It was a good short sale at 15 because in December it declined to 5. At no time after it left 76 in July did it ever show anything but down trend. Therefore, the correct way to trade would have been to sell it short at any price.

You must learn to forget about the high or low price at which a stock has sold. I have not picked out International Combustion Engineering as a lone example in the 1929 decline. There are hundreds of others. Advance Rumely is another stock that sold up to 105 in May 1929, and declined to 7 in November 1929. I could pick out many other stocks for you that never sold higher than 25 or 30 during 1929, and declined to 15, 10, and 5. A stock is a cinch short sale at any price so long as the trend is down, and it is good to buy at any price so long as the trend is up.

DANGEROUS SHORT SALES

The stocks that are most dangerous to sell short are those with a very small volume or those that have a small floating supply. These stocks are closely held and can be easily cornered. It is certainly easier to cause a bigger advance in a stock with one million shares outstanding than it is in a stock with 10 to 50 million shares. Pick the stocks with small volume of shares for purchases and when you sell short, sell the stocks with the largest volume of stock outstanding.

Some of the stocks with a small number of shares outstanding which have had big advances are, Baldwin Locomotive, Crucible Steel, Houston Oil, U. S. Cast Iron Pipe and Vanadium Steel.

BUYING LOW-PRICED STOCKS LATE IN A BULL CAMPAIGN

When stocks have gone up for many years it is only natural that traders begin to pick stocks to follow, which have not advanced. They pick low-priced stocks that they think will go up because other stocks have gone up. This is one of the greatest mistakes that could be made. If a bull campaign has run for several years and general indications are that it is nearing the end, that is, within the last 3 to 6 months of the end, it is very dangerous to buy low-priced stocks expecting them to move in the last section of the bull campaign. While some low-priced stocks are late movers, as a rule, the high-priced stocks are used to finish in the final grand rush of a bull campaign. Only buy low-priced stocks when they show by your chart that they have advanced into new high levels and are in strong position, otherwise as long as they are in a narrow trading range and inactive, leave them alone. The following list of low-priced stocks not only failed to advance in the latter part of the 1929 Bull Campaign, but they went down while other stocks were going up, and traders who bought them suffered heavy losses: Ajax Rubber, American Agricultural Chemical, American Beet Sugar, American La France, American Ship & Commerce, Armour A, Booth Fisheries, Callahan Zinc & Lead, Consolidated Textile, Dome Mines, Electric Boat, Guantanamo Sugar, Jordan Motors, Kelly Springfield, Kelvinator, Louisiana Oil, Loft, Moon Motors, Omnibus, Panhandle Producers, Park Utah, Reo Motors, Reynolds Spring, Snider Packing, Submarine Boat, Ward Baking B, Wilson & Company.

HOW TO DETERMINE TEMPORARY LEADERS

If you will get the daily paper and look over it every day after the market closes and then pick the stocks which had the largest volume of sales that day, you will be able to determine the ones that are the leaders at that particular time and will be for at least a few days to follow, or longer. Watch the stocks that have very small volume for a long period of time and remain in a narrow trading range. Then as soon as the volume increases, watch which way the stock starts to move and go with the trend. When a stock suddenly becomes very active on a large volume of sales, you can consider that at least it will be a leader temporarily and should go with it.

SLOW MOVING STOCKS

There are certain stocks that move slowly for a long time, but as long as the trend is up, you can expect this class of stocks to finally finish with a fast move up. It pays to wait to buy or sell until the last fast move or final grand rush, up or down, comes. The big money is made in these fast moves, some of which last 3 to 10 days, others much longer. As a general rule, after a stock has had a fast move up or down for 6 to 7 weeks, as the case maybe, you can expect it to change trend, at least temporarily. For example, note the moves in U. S. Steel, U. S. Industrial Alcohol and Timken Roller Bearing in July and August 1929. All of these stocks were late movers and reached the boiling point in August.

WHY STOCKS GO TO EXTREMES

The market does not fool you. You fool yourself. Stocks go to extreme high or low levels, or, in other words, they go too high or too low. The reason for this is that traders wait until stocks have had big declines and they have big losses; then they all sell at once and stocks are carried below normal or intrinsic values. Again, in the last stage of a bull market, when everybody gets over-optimistic and have made big profits, they increase their trading and buy in large volume regardless of price. Shorts, after suffering losses, get to where they are afraid to sell short, and the market has a wild, runaway advance, which eliminates the short interest and increases the long interest and leaves the stocks in a weak technical position, from which a sharp decline follows.

WHY STOCKS MOVE SLOWLY AT LOW LEVELS AND FAST AT HIGH LEVELS

The higher a stock goes, the faster the move and the bigger the opportunities for profits. The reason for this is that most of the public's buying and selling is at low levels. After a stock has been at a low level, say 25 or lower, for a long number of years and the public has bought a large amount of it, it advances to around 50 and people buy more. When it reaches 100 or around this figure, they either all sell out or the public gets overconfident and comes in and buys so much stock that it has a big decline. When the public takes profits, the insiders and strong financial interests have to buy the stock. They buy it because they know that it is worth more and going to sell higher later. When the public selling is all absorbed, it is easier for the insiders to mark the stock up fast, because they do not encounter heavy selling. When a stock gets around 180 to 200, there is always a lot of short covering, and the pools, who bought the stock at lower levels, sell out and take profits. The general public does not trade in stocks above 200 per share. Therefore, after a stock crosses this level, it is a fight between the professional short sellers and the strong financial interests who are backing it. A stock can move from 200 to 300 in less time than it takes it to move from 50 to 100, because the people who are trading in it are large traders and buy or sell large amounts. Of course, every stock must reach a level where the insiders will sell enough stock to check the advance and turn the main trend down. Then comes the big opportunity for the man who will sell a high-priced stock short, but he must wait until his charts show that the main trend has turned down.

Low-priced stocks, or stocks selling below 50 and 25, sometimes have a very fast move down. A stock like New Haven, which at one time sold at 280 and gradually worked lower, had some of its fastest declines below 100 and also some sharp, swift declines below 50. It finally had a wide-open break after it was selling at 25. The cause for this was selling by those who had held the stock for years and saw it work lower year after year and their capital shrink, with no dividends on the stock, and they gave up hope and sold out. A large majority of stockholders sold New Haven between 20 and 12. Then, after a long period of dullness and accumulation, New Haven started to come back and advanced from 10 to 132, in October 1929.

TIME LIMIT TO HOLD STOCKS

When you make a trade, it must be for a good reason, and for possibilities of profit in a reasonable length of time, but remember that you can be wrong, and if the stock goes against you, the loss must be stopped. You can be wrong also when the stock does not go against you. If it remains stationary, you are losing interest on your money, and this is an actual loss, because with that same amount of money, you can grasp a new opportunity and make money. The average stock, after it shows an indication of going up or down, should continue to move within 3 weeks, if it is going to move at all. Therefore, about 3 weeks' time is the limit that you should wait for a movement to start. If it does not start, get out and look for a new opportunity. Some slow moving stocks like investment issues will hold 3 to 4 months in a trading range. Therefore, in some cases, it pays to wait 2 or 3 months for a move to get under way. You must remember that the longer you hold a stock that does not move, the more your judgment gets warped, because you are holding on hope. Study the facts and get all of the reasons why the stock is not moving, and if you do not find some good reason why it should move in a limited length of time, do not hold it; get out. If you find some good cause or reason, which you think should move the stock in a limited length of time and it fails to work, there is some thing wrong and the stock may move in the opposite direction. You should make it a rule that on the first indication of being wrong, you should immediately get out of a stock. Your judgment is always much better out of the market than when you are in, because you have no hopes and fears.

MANIPULATED STOCKS

Many times stocks are advanced far beyond their intrinsic values simply because some pools can control the stocks for a short time and manipulate them beyond all reason, then a collapse follows. Therefore, the trader should know what to do if he happens to get caught in a stock of this kind, because there is just as much money in trading in a stock that is manipulated, as long as it is going up, as there is in one that is advancing on merit, but the object is to get out at the right time and always go with the trend.

Advance Rumely - This was a stock that had a phenomenal advance in 1928 and 1929, which was not warranted by the earnings and was mostly manipulation. However, the investor or trader who followed the chart and indications could have made a lot of money in it. A review of its past history would have helped the trader to know when to sell. 1912 high 101; 1915 low $1.00 per share; 1919 high 54; 1924 low 6, which showed that this stock was a late mover and made bottom several years later than 1920 and 1921 when most of the stocks made bottom and started up. From 6 in 1924, Advance Rumely rallied to 22 in 1926. It declined in 1927 to 7, which was a buying level, because it was down within one point of the 1924 low. A big advance followed from this low price, and in April 1928, it crossed 16, which showed higher prices and was an indication that the trader should buy more stock. In the same month it crossed 22, the high of 1926, getting into a strong position as it was above all of the highs since 1921. In September 1928, advanced to 64; then followed a decline to December 1928, when the stock sold at 31. From this level a rapid advance followed and in about 5 months' time the stock advanced to 105, up 74 which was moving entirely too fast and the price not being warranted by earnings or any condition in the company, could not hold. Therefore, the trader should have known that 1912 high was 101 and should have sold out around this price. However, the stock went 4 points higher. If he had not sold out at this price, he should have been following the stock up with a 10-point stop loss order, or 10 points from the high. This would have put him out of the market at 95. After the stock declined to 95 it never rallied, went right on down, and when it broke 82, was under 3 weeks' bottoms, which indicated much lower prices. About the time the stock sold at 105, there were tips out all over the country to buy, but from that time on it acted very badly and showed that it was a complete collapse; rallies were very small and the trader who got caught had no chance to get out and many of them did get caught with the stock. In October 1929, it again sold at 7, down to the same level of 1927, which was a buying level. After that it rallied to 23, and the trader had a chance to make a quick profit. Since that time it has held in a narrow trading range.

Now, the fact that this stock had a collapse at a time when there were no big breaks in other stocks showed that it was manipulation. Of course, from September, 1929, on, when all stocks declined in the panic, the good went with the bad, but when a stock goes against the trend, as Advance Rumely did, it is an indication that there is something wrong and that it has been manipulated to unreasonably high prices, and traders should beware.

STOCKS THAT HAVE BIG ADVANCES

Volcanic eruptions are far apart. Vesuvius is in eruption every day but only a minor eruption. The big eruptions and destructive disturbances have only occurred about every 20 years. It is the same with stocks. These fast moves and big eruptions only happen at rare intervals. Go over the list of stocks which have been leaders in the past and you will see how far apart these big moves are. For example:

Union Pacific - From the low of 80 in 1904, this stock advanced to 195 in 1905 and 1906; declined to 100 in the panic of 1907, and advanced to 219 in September 1909.
This was what I call a volcanic eruption in a stock. It had its first big advance in 1906; then went higher in 1900. After that, it worked lower without having any big moves until 1917 when it declined to 102 and in 1921 made 111. From 1921 to 1928, it advanced slowly, never having any fast runaway moves. In August 1928, Union Pacific was selling at 194; then started up and crossed the high level of 219, the top of 1909. After crossing this level, it declined to 209 on March 26, 1929; then gradually worked up until July, 1929, when a fast advance started from 232. It continued to work higher until August 1929, when it reached 297, the highest level in its history, being up 103 points from the low of August 1928. This is what I call a volcanic eruption in a stock and when it comes, it is time to sell out, because the big opportunity has passed. The man that traded in Union Pacific after 1909 and hoped for it to make fast moves up like it did in 1906 and 1909, had to wait over 20 years for another opportunity of this kind. Therefore, you must learn that when once a stock has a rapid advance of this kind it will not have another one like it for a long period of time and it may never have another big advance.

Crucible Steel - This is another stock which had a volcanic eruption. It started up in 1915 from around 13 and advanced to 110; then reacted to around 45; started up in 1919 from around 54 and advanced to 278 in April 1920. It was then split up and a stock dividend declared. The stock worked lower until it reached 48 in 1924. The man who traded in Crucible from 1924 to 1929, hoping for it to have another advance like 1919 and 1920 missed big profits in other stocks which had advances similar to Crucible.

Therefore, you must always watch for the new leaders and leave the old leaders alone, once they have had their big advances. The same occurs after a prolonged decline It will be a long period of time before the stock will have another similar big break and it will probably be slow on the next advance.

NEW STOCKS

Remember that it is always safer to sell new stocks short. By new stocks, I mean those that have only been listed from a few months to 2 years on the New York Stock Exchange or the stocks of newly organized companies which have been distributed. At the time the underwriters are distributing the stock, the news is so bullish that the people who buy the stock hope for too much, but in a few months or few years they realize that they expected more than was possible. The result is a period of liquidation, reorganization or reconstruction. There is a shake out of the week and speculative long interest, and then the stock starts up from a permanent foundation, because it has been bought by investors and by big interests who will hold on from low levels after the speculators who bought at high levels are out. When such stocks reach bottom, it often requires a long period for accumulation to take place.

FACTS YOU NEVER HEAR ABOUT SHORT SELLING

One of the reasons why so many people are afraid to sell stocks short is because they never hear the truth about the short side and are never taught that it is just as safe to sell short as it is to buy stocks and that they can make profits much faster in a bear market than they do in a bull market. Every newspaper writer, investment service, and broker, as a general rule, discourages short selling. Banks advise against it. Why all of this talk against short selling when stocks always go down when they get too high? You will often read in the newspaper the following: "Bears stampeded," "Bears trapped," "Shorts squeezed," "Bears forced to cover," "Bears put to rout," "Shorts will be punished," "A certain stock is harboring a large short interest." Now, why do you never hear the newspapers talking the opposite, or in other words, say, "Bulls squeezed," "Bulls put to rout," "Bulls forced to liquidate," "Preparing to run out the bulls"?

When stocks were at the bottom at the time of the 1929 panic, the New York Stock Exchange called for a list of short sellers. When the market was at the top and so dangerous, when everybody was buying and needed warning and protection, why did not the Exchange call for a list of the people who were buying stocks and also get a list of the people who were selling stocks at these high levels and warn the public? It is just as important to have the names of people who are long of stocks at the top and know who is supplying them as it is to know who is selling them short at the bottom. But neither report would do any good. When everybody is wrong and long at the top, stocks have to go down, and when at the bottom everybody has liquidated and there is a short interest, they go up. The average trader hears everything to discourage him against selling short and gets all of the good news about buying and how it pays to buy. But what the trader or investor wants to know, is the truth and the facts and not things which are based on sentiment and hope.

Any man who will study the records of high and low prices over a long period of years will be forced to the conclusion that short selling is just as safe as buying for long account, provided he sells short at the right time. Some of the "lambs" who lost their fleece in the first and second battle of Bull run on October 24 and 29, 1929, certainly know that they would have been much better off if they had sold short. During the October panic the bulls and lambs made the most disastrous retreat in history. The bulls were demoralized and put to rout after the second battle of Bull run, on October 29, bull horns, hides, hoofs, heels, and tails were strewn from Wall Street to Water Street, and from the Battery to the Bronx. Lambs limped home with their voices keyed to a note of pain exclaiming, "Of all sad suckers that have ever bit, we have a sneaking idea that we are it." The bulls followed in the train and bellowed, "never again." Bull blood flowed like rain from the Battery to Maiden Lane. It was Lawson's dream of "Friday the 13th" made real. Why after all this slaughter of the lambs and the breaking of the heart of the bulls, did we not hear anything said about the terrible slaughter of the bulls? We began to hear more talk about shorts going to be squeezed and shorts run in. If there had been more short sellers in the panicky decline of October and November 1929, stocks would not have gone down as low, because shorts would have covered on the way down and would have helped to support the market and prevented a disastrous wide-open break in many stocks. Short selling is just as essential to a healthy market as buying for a long account is at the right time.

WHY ARE STOCKS SPLIT UP AND STOCK DIVIDENDS DECLARED?

It is a well known fact, as I have stated before, that the public, as a general rule do not trade, to a large extent, in stocks selling above $100 per share and when stocks get above $200 and $300 per share the public's participation in the trading gets less and less. The object of most companies in listing their stocks on the New York Stock Exchange is to provide a ready public market and to assure a wide distribution of their stocks. Therefore, in order to get the public to buy stocks after they are at high levels, they are split up and stock dividends declared so the stocks will again sell at $100 per share or lower. Then the public can and will buy them. Many good companies declare stock dividends and split up their stock for the good and sufficient reason that stock dividends are not taxable under the existing laws; others declare stock dividends because they really want the public to have a chance to participate in their companies and become partners with them and share in the profits. However, many highly manipulated stocks are split up and dividends declared for the sole purpose of selling the stocks to the public and after they are sold to the public and distributed, then they decline to much lower levels.

As a general rule, after a stock is split up, it requires quite a time for it to be distributed or accumulated, and often after a dividend is declared the stock does not have any big move. Of course, determine the position of the stock by your charts and trade accordingly, but a good rule to follow is that after a stock has had a big advance and a stock dividend has been declared, get out of it and leave it alone; look for another opportunity and watch that stock until it shows it is ready for a big move one way or the other.

WHO OWNS THE COMPANY

One of the very important things for you to know about a stock you trade in is who owns the controlling interest in the company and who manages it. The stocks which J. P. Morgan & Co. have been interested in or manage, have always made good, because this company does not put its money into a company unless they believe it has great future possibilities. The corporations in which the du Ponts have become interested have all made good. Therefore, when you are seeking to become a partner in a corporation, go in with the successful men but of course get in at the right time. The time to have bought U.S. Steel was not when the corporation was first organized but when the stock declined to around 10 and showed that it had made final bottom. The fact that J. P. Morgan & Co. was in it showed that it would eventually make good. Although U. S. Steel has broken back 50 to 75 points many times from its top levels, it has always gone higher later. The charts have always shown when it was top for a decline and bottom for another advance.

In 1921, when the Morgan and du Pont interests took over General Motors from Durant, the stock was selling around 15 and continued to decline to 8¼ and remained in a narrow, trading range until 1924, when the main trend turned up. After you knew that the company was controlled by Morgan and the du Ponts, you should have watched for a chance to buy, because there was every indication that they would make the company a success, but there was no need to hurry. You could have waited three years and then bought near the bottom and made fast money.

National City Bank, one of the largest banks in the world, has in recent years become interested in many corporations, and these corporations are all making a success, but there will come a time when their stocks will be top and should be sold out. When bottom is reached and the charts show that the trend is turning up again, it will pay you to buy the stocks in the companies that the large financial interests in this country are interested in.

Bad management has wrecked many a good company. It was always claimed that Jay Gould wrecked the railroads before he started to build them up. It used to be a favorite saying with professional traders "sell the Gould stocks." Erie was another company that was badly managed over a long period of years. The stock was watered. The public lost all the money they put into it several times, as the company went into the hands of receivers several times.

The late E. H. Harriman took over the Union Pacific in 1896 when it was bankrupt and made it one of the greatest railroads in the United States. It has paid 10 per cent dividends for over 24 years. Harriman was a constructive builder, and the investors who bought into the concerns that he managed have made money. Bad management can wreck a good company and good management can make a bad company prosperous.

MONEY RATES, BOND AN STOCK PRICES

It is important to study and compare money rates, average bond prices, and also average stock prices. You will see how money rates influence bond prices and how highs and lows for bond prices vary from average stock prices. The money rates forecast a decline or advance in bond prices, and the bond prices forecast what will later follow in the stock market.

The chart on money rates for a long period of years shows you what high call money rates mean and what low money rates mean. There has never been a period of high money but what lower prices for stocks followed sooner or later. High money rates mean that loans have increased, that the supply of money is getting scarce, and that sooner or later speculators will be forced to liquidate stocks to repay loans. Low interest rates do not always mean that a bull market is coming or that stocks will advance. Extremely cheap money means just the opposite of extremely high money - that there is very little demand. Business is usually bad when money is cheap or, at least, when rates are below normal. Therefore, when business is bad, stocks will not show large earnings and dividends cannot be increased. When business starts to improve and money rates gradually advance, stocks will move with the money market or slightly ahead of it.

In December 1914, average stock prices reached low, and in September 1915, average bond prices reached low, or about 9 months later than the low levels reached on stocks. In November 1915, stock prices reached high, and in January 1916, bond prices reached higher levels. After that there was no rally in bond prices. They continued to decline until December 1917, when low levels were reached. Stocks did have rallies in 1917 and U. S. Steel made extreme high of the year in May. In December 1917, stocks reached low levels. In May 1918, bonds were top, but this was only a small rally and in September 1918, bonds made the same low as in December 1917. This is what we call a double bottom and a place to buy. At this time stocks were holding up and working higher. In November 1918, bonds made the last high of the rally and started working lower. Stocks had a big boom in 1919 and reached top in November, when bonds were working lower.

Final high for stocks was reached one year later than the high for bonds. In May 1920, bonds reached final low and in December 1920, stocks reached low for a rally. Bonds made top of rally in October 1920, from which there was a sharp decline to a second low in December 1920.Top of rally in the stock market was made in May 1921. Top of a rally in the bond market culminated in January 1921; last low for bonds was reached in June 1921, which was a second higher bottom made one year later than the final low. Some stocks made low in June 1921, but the average list reached low in August 1921, which was the final bottom from which the big bull campaign started. This was 16 months later than the low on bonds. Bonds reached high in September 1922, and stocks continued to advance until March 1923, when they reached higher levels for a reaction. Bonds reached low of the reaction in March 1923, at the same time that stocks reached high, and the bonds held in a narrow range for many months and made last low in October 1923. Stocks also made a low in October 1923; then rallied to February 1924, and made last low in May 1924, although some stocks did not make low until October 1924, and started up soon after Mr. Coolidge was elected President of the United States.

While stocks were having this last reaction, bonds were slowly working higher. In February 1926, stocks made top and a big break followed in March. In August 1926, stocks made a higher top, followed by a sharp decline in October 1926. Bonds made high in May 1926, and held in a narrow range with a small reaction until October, when they reached the last low and started up. In January and April 1928, bonds made final high, just above 99. Failing to reach 100 indicated that there were probably heavy selling orders around 100 and no doubt many people failed to get out of bonds at the right time, whereas if they had been keeping a chart and watching how bonds held for several months without making any important gain in price, they would have known that there was heavy selling and should have sold out because money rates were getting higher. The bond trend turned down in April 1928; reached bottom for a small rally in August 1928, and the rally ended in November 1928; while stocks continued to advance to September 3, 1929, when final high was reached about 20 months later than bonds had made top. However, it is important to know that the average on all stocks on the New York Stock Exchange made extreme high in November 1928. In August 1929, bonds made low, but went slightly lower in October 1929; then rallied in December 1929; had a small reaction in January 1930, and went higher in April 1930. Watch money rates and the bond market, as you will find them helpful in determining the trend of stock prices.

CHAPTER VI
HOW INVESTORS SHOULD TRADE

The big money in many stocks is made by taking a long pull position, but there are times when it does not pay to hold stocks for the long pull, depending upon the cycle which the market is in and how near the market is to a distributing stage. Suppose you buy a medium or low-priced stock to hold for the long pull, and one which pays no dividends; you must figure the interest on the money which you have invested, and unless you make profits enough to pay the interest and more too, it does not pay to take a long pull position. Many people buy a low-priced stock and hold it for several years, then finally sell with 5 points' profit and think that they have made money, but if they will figure the compound interest on the money invested over the period of time, they will find that they have not made good interest on their money and, at the same time, have risked their capital.

WHEN INVESTORS SHOULD TAKE PROFITS

When I speak of investors, I mean long pull traders or those who buy stocks to hold for several years. Investors must have some reliable guide to get in near the bottom of a decline, then when they get in right, they should hold until the bull campaign ends, ignoring minor fluctuations, but studying the charts of a stock to determine when it shows weakness and watching for a sign of the end in order to sell out their investments.

New York Central - In TRUTH OF THE STOCK TAPE, on page 95, which was written in the early part of 1923, I picked New York Central as one of the best stocks for an investor or trader to buy. Examine a chart of this stock from the low in June 1921, to the top in September 1929, showing the important swings and reactions, all of which indicated up trend. There were progressive higher tops, and higher bottoms all the way up. Now, the important thing for the investor to watch was for the best selling point. My rule says to watch for the final grand rush and a boiling movement which may last anywhere from 7 to 10 weeks. From a low of 65 in June 1921, New York Central advanced to 101 in October 1922. In November reacted to 89 down 12 points. In June 1923, sold at 104 and in July reacted to 96, down 8 points. December 1923, high 108, reacted to 100, down 8 points. During February, March and April 1924, it held at 100; then advanced to a new high level, which indicated much higher prices. In February 1925, reached high at 125; reacted in March and June to 114, down 11 points, still not as much reaction as it had from the first top in 1922 and showing up trend. In December 1925; it sold at 136 and in March 1926, when there was a panic in most stocks, it declined to 117, down 19 points, but failing to break the low of 114 made in 1925 and making a higher bottom still showed strong up trend. Therefore, the investor should have held on and not sold out the stock.

In September 1926, made a new high at 147; reacted to 130 in October, down only 17 points, not as much as the reaction in March 1926, and still showing up trend. Therefore, the investor should have ignored this reaction and held his stock. October 1927, high 171; February 1928, low 156, down 15 points, still showing up trend; May 1928, high 191, a new high. In July 1928, it reacted to 160, down 31 points, the biggest reaction at any time since 1921 and a warning that selling pressure was getting heavier. However, the stock failed to get to 156, the low of February 1928, and showed that the main trend was still up, because at no time had it broken a previous bottom or Resistance Level from which the upward movement had started. February 1929, high 204; March and April 1929, low 179, down

25 points, failing to react as much as it did in July 1928. From this level followed the final grand rush to September 1929, when the stock sold at 257, up 78 points in 4 months.

Now, we will presume that the investor did not know that the panic was coming in September and October 1929, so he could not sell out at the top. In order to determine when to sell or where to place a stop loss order, he should look back and find the greatest reaction from any top which was 31 points from the top in May 1928, at 191 to the low of 160 in July, 1928. The next decline of importance was 25 points, from February 1929, to March and April 1929. A good rule to follow is: After a stock has had its final grand rush and reached the boiling point, a stop loss order should be placed an equal distance from the final top, or the same number of points as the last reaction. Therefore, the investor would have had a stop, 25 points down from the top. Then when it sold at 257 the stop loss order would have been at 232. After this price was reached the stock never had a big rally until it declined to 160 in November 1929, down 97 points. This was again a buying level because it was down 100 points and to the price from which the advance started in July 1928. The low was 156 in February 1928, so if the investor bought again at 160 he should have placed a stop at 155 just under the last low level. New York Central advanced to 192 in February 1930, and the low in March 1930, was 181 and the low in February, 178. Therefore, the investor should have a stop at 177 on the stock as it stands, at the time of this writing, March 1930.

If an investor had followed my rules laid down in TRUTH OF THE STOCK TAPE and had bought New York Central around 65 and 66 in 1921 and followed it up according to the rules we have just given, he would have been out at 232 on a stop and would have a profit of 167 points or $16,700 and all during the time he held the stock the dividends paid a good return on his invested capital. Suppose the stock cost him originally $6,500 for 100 shares; then when it sold at 130, where he had a profit of $6,500, suppose he bought 100 shares more, his profits would have been $23,200, or nearly four times his original capital or 400 per cent on his investment in a little over 8 years, or a gain of about 50 per cent per year, which proves that long pull trading pays. Of course, by pyramiding and buying the stock every 15 or 20 points up, the profits would have been much greater, but the investor is not supposed to pyramid. The speculator-investor or trader takes greater risks and pyramids closer together when the market is moving his way.

WHAT INVESTORS SHOULD WATCH

A man who is trading for the long pull and is really an investor should watch the big swings, the extent of the reactions, and the time or duration of the reactions.

The investor must first pick the right stock according to the rules to buy and then follow the trend as long as it is up. Then when the trend changes and turns down, he should get out and leave that stock alone, and look for opportunities in a new stock which has not had a big advance.

Southern Railway - The yearly chart will show you that the high on Southern Railway in 1902 was 41; then it declined to 17 in 1903, and in 1906 made top at 42, just one point above the top of 1902. The low in 1907 and 1908 was 10; high in 1909 was 34, and the three following years made tops around 33 to 32. It declined in 1915, reaching a low of 13, advanced to 36 in 1916, getting only 2 points above the 1909 high. Then, during 1917, 1918, 1919 and 1920, tops were made around 34 and 33, from which a decline followed and bottoms were made at 18 in 1920, 1921 and 1922. Holding for

3 years at these same levels and making a higher bottom than in 1915, the stock indicated that it was going higher. In 1922 when it crossed 24, the high of 1921, it indicated higher prices. Then, in 1923, when it crossed 36, which was above all tops since 1906, this was another indication for a big advance and that it would be an early leader.

In the early part of 1924 Southern Railway crossed 42, the high of 1906, which was the highest in its history. Crossing this top 18 years later was a sure sign for a big advance, and the trader who had already bought at lower levels should have bought more and pyramided on the way up. It advanced to 165 in 1928 and declined to 109 in November 1929. Study the stocks that make years of tops and then start making higher bottoms and finally cross the extreme high levels and get into new territory. They are the ones that investors and traders can make big profits in. On page 97 of TRUTH OF THE STOCK TAPE, written in early 1923, you can see that I picked American Can, Rock Island and Southern Railway for big advances. These stocks all made good, and if you apply the same rules to stocks in similar position, you will be able to select the proper stocks in the future that possess possibilities for big advances.

One of the things which the investor should not do is to buy in new companies unless he is sure of their future, and he cannot always be sure of it. The biggest and the best men make mistakes and most of them become overoptimistic at the time a new company starts and expect greater things than are ever realized. Therefore, the safest rule for the investor to follow in making long pull investments is to buy the old or seasoned stocks. If a stock is over 20 years old and has a fairly good dividend record, he should look up its record and buy it at the time it is low according to the chart and wait for the final grand rush to sell. The reason that these old or seasoned stocks move fast in their final stages is because after a long period of years nearly all of the stock gets into the hands of investors and the floating supply is very small; therefore, when a great buying demand starts, the stock moves up fast until it reaches a level where investors will sell in large amounts and check the advance.

Atchison - In TRUTH OF THE STOCK TAPE, we refer to Atchison as being one of the good railroads to buy in 1921. This company was incorporated in 1895; therefore it was 26 years old in 1921 and had a good dividend record. In June 1921, the low on Atchison was 76; September 1922, high 108; November 1922, low 98, down 10 points; March 1923, high 105; October 1923, low 94, down 14 points from 108. Failing to break 3 points under these bottoms, still showed the main trend up. March 1925, high 127; June 1925, low 117, down 10 points; December 1925, high 140; March 1926, low 122, down 18 points. This was a small decline considering that this was a panic and that some high-priced stocks declined 100 points. Atchison still showed a strong position and the investor should have held it. September 1926, high 161; October 1926, low 142, down 19 points. Main trend still up and the investor should hold. April 1927, high 201. My rule says that always around 100, 200 and 300 or the round figures stocks meet with heavy selling and have some reaction. The investor knowing this could have sold out and bought Atchison cheaper. However, he did not know that the trend had turned and the chart did not show it.

In June 1927, it declined to 181, down 20 points, still making a higher bottom and showing up trend. December 1927, high 201, the same as April. Here again the investor could have sold out, but the trend had not turned down. March 1928, low 183, down 18 points, still making a higher bottom and showing up trend. The investor at this time should have had a stop at 178, or 3 points under the previous low level. April 1928, high 197, making a slightly lower top. June 1928, low 184, down 13 points. If the investor placed a stop loss order 3 points under the low of March 1928, he still would have been safe and here for the third time Atchison made a higher bottom, showing that when it could make a higher top it would go much higher. February 1929, 209 high, a new high and an indication of much higher prices. March 1929, low 196, down 13 points, exactly the same reaction as the previous one. August 1929, high 298. Failing to cross 300, the even figure, was an indication of making top, besides Atchison had had the final grand rush. The last two reaction points were 13 points, therefore, the trader would have followed up with a stop loss order 13 points under the high price. This would have put him out of the market at 285. In November 1929, Atchison declined to 200, down 98 points from the top, another buying level, because it was down nearly 100 points and at the same time holding 2 points above the low of March 1929.

If the investor bought around 200, he should have placed a stop loss order about 5 points away. In March 1930, it advanced to 242 and the stop at this writing should be at 227 under the low of February 1930. One of the reasons why 200 was a buying level in November 1929, was because Atchison held for 5 months from January to May 1929, making bottoms around 196. The fact that people bought stock at 196 previously showed that there was strong support and again when it stopped at 200 showed that there was somebody still willing to buy all the stock offered at a slightly higher level, which indicated that it was the proper place to buy for at least a rally.

American Telephone & Telegraph Co.- This stock proved to be a great investment in 1920 and has paid enormous profits and big dividends since. It had a big advance with only small reactions. One of the reasons why the old or seasoned stocks have such small reactions is because they are held by investors who do not sell on rallies or get scared and sell out on declines like the professional traders who trade in stocks that the public buy on margin. Buy these good old dividend-payers at low accumulative levels, but not near the top.

As American Telephone & Telegraph is an old company, it is important to review its high and low prices for years back. The high in 1902 was 186; low in the panic of 1907 was 88; next high was in 1911, when it reached 153; next low in 1913 was 110 and in 1916 high 134; 1918 low 91. Now, this was a strong buying level because at the time of the panic in 1907 the stock declined to 88. Therefore, it should be bought anywhere close to this level with a stop loss order at 85, or 3 points under the old low level. It is important to study the tops: February, 1918, high 108; August low 91; October high 108; December low 98; March 1919, high 108; April low 101; June high 108; December low 95; March 1920, high 100; July low 92; September high 100; December low 95. Note the lows in 1919 and 1920 were higher than the low level reached in August 1918, showing good support and a buying level.

There were four tops around 108, and in May 1921, the stock advanced to 108 again, but it only reacted to 102 in July 1921, again making a higher bottom, showing strong support. Now, if you had bought stock near the bottom and wanted to pyramid, the place to buy more would have been when it crossed 110, getting above the tops at 108. The stock continued to work higher each year, making higher tops and higher bottoms, showing that the main trend was up. In May 1928, it sold at 210 and in July 1928, reacted to 172, failing to break enough under the low level of November 1927, to show that the trend had turned down. If the investor had been watching the stock, or the trader had been waiting for an opportunity to buy in December 1924, he would have bought more at 132 because at this time it was over the tops of 1922, 1923, and 1924. The final grand rush occurred from May 1929, to September 1929, when the stock advanced from 205 to 310, up 105 points. This was the final grand rush and the place for the investor to sell out his stock, especially as the last move was 105 points, but the investor or trader could not know when the exact high would be reached, therefore, he should look back to the last reaction and place a stop loss order this distance away. The last reaction was 33 points, from 238 in April 1929, to May 1929, when the stock sold at 205. This would have put the investor out at 277, and if he had bought around 100, he would have nothing to worry about, even if he missed 33 points at the top of the final grand rush.

It declined to 198 in November 1929. This was a buying level, because it was 110 points down from the top and there is always support around the even figure when the stock declines to 200 or when it advances to around this level. If the investor bought again around this figure, he should watch for the reaction point to place a stop loss order. The stock advanced to 235 in December 1929, and reacted to 215 in January 1930, a no-point reaction. It advanced to 274 in April 1930. Therefore, the investor should follow up with a stop loss order 20 points away, or until he gets a better indication to sell. In view of the fact that American Tel. & Tel. has had a final grand rush, the investor should not expect it to go back to 310 again, at least for many years to come.

People's Gas - Study the yearly high and low chart from 1895 to 1930. In 1899 the high was 130 and in 1907 low 70; in 1913 the stock again advanced to 130, the high of 1899.
Notice that the low levels from 1909 to 1917 were between 100 and 106, which showed that during all these years there was good support around 100. The trend had been up for years and investors had gained great confidence in this stock. When it broke 100 in 1918, this was an indication that something was wrong. Investors should have sold out and traders should have gone short. The stock declined to 27 in 1920. Big accumulation took place and the trend turned up again. In 1926 it crossed 130, the high of 1899 and 1913; crossing this level was an indication of much higher prices, and investors and traders should have bought more of it. A big advance followed and in 1929 the stock reached a high of 404, when a stock dividend was declared.

U. S. Steel Swings - I use U. S. Steel for an example in many cases, not because my theory or rules cannot be proved by other stocks, but because Steel is one of the best known stocks to the general public and they understand more about its movements. Examine a swing chart showing the major and minor movements on Steel from the date of listing on the New York Stock Exchange, March 28, 1901, to April 7, 1930. It started at 42 ½ in March 1901, and advanced to 55 in April. Being a new stock with volume of five million shares, naturally it took a long time to distribute it. The first big decline occurred in the panic of May 9, 1901, when the stock declined to 24. In July it rallied to 48; declined to 37, and in January 1902, advanced to 46. Failing to reach the previous top of 48 showed good selling and an investor or trader should have sold out and gone short. In December 1902, it declined to 30; in March 1903, advanced to 39, still making a lower top than the previous top. In May 1904, it declined to 8⅜, the lowest price in history. Around this level there was accumulation about 8 or 10 months. Investors should have bought around this low level or when it crossed 13 in September 1904, which was over the Resistance Level made between November 1903, and August 1904. In April 1905, made high at 38. Failing to cross the high of March 1903 indicated a reaction. In May 1905, declined to 25, where it received good support and indicated a buying point. February 1906, advanced to 50, getting only 2 points above the high of July 1901; July 1906, reacted to 33; January 1907, advanced to 50. Failing to cross the high of 1906 indicated that the stock should be sold out and sold short, especially as the stock was still below the high level made in April 1901. In the panic of March 1907, Steel declined to 32 and in July 1907, advanced to 39, still making lower tops, and in the panic of October 1907, declined to 22. This was a buying level because it was just under the low level reached in May 1905. A rapid advance followed and reactions were very small. Steel advanced to 58¾ in November 1908. This was the highest point in its history, crossing the levels of 1906 and 1907 and the high of April 1901, and giving indication that it was getting ready to go very much higher. Therefore, it was a purchase on all reactions.

In February 1909, Steel declined to 41⅛. A study of the weekly high and low chart will show that it indicated bottom and should have been bought. A big advance followed and at no time did Steel react over 5 points until it advanced to 94⅞ in October 1909, where there was the heaviest volume of trading of any time in history and the weekly and monthly high and low charts showed that it was making top. Suppose an investor or trader bought near the bottom, in February 1909, or at any previous low level. After the February reaction in 1909, if he had followed the stock up with a stop loss order 5 to 7 points away, the stop would have never been caught. The trader who was watching for reactions to buy, after seeing the first reaction of 5 points, could have bought every time it reacted 5 points with a stop loss order 3 points away, and his stop would never have been caught. In this way big profits could have been made pyramiding.

From the top in October 1909, Steel declined to 75 in February 1910; rallied to 89 in March; declined to 62 in July, advanced to 81 in November; then declined to 70 in December 1910, and rallied again to 82 in February 1911. Note that it was making lower tops and lower bottoms all the time. The fact that it made three tops around 81 to 82 indicated that it was a short sale at these levels with a stop 3 points away. In April 1911, it declined to 73 and again in May 1911, advanced to 81, again failing to cross the high levels of November 1909, and the high of February 1911. A sharp decline followed and in November 1911, when the United States Government filed suit to dissolve the United States Steel Corporation, the stock declined to 50. This was a buying level because during 1901, 1906, and 1907 Steel had made tops at 50. Therefore, the old Resistance Level for a top would become a buying level when it declined to the same level. From this level Steel advanced to 70 in December 1911, where there was good selling and a reaction followed to February, 1912, when it declined to 59, making a higher bottom and indicating a buying point for a rally. In April 1912, it advanced to 73 and in May 1912, declined to 65, again getting support at a higher level, showing that it should rally again. In October 1912, advanced to 80, again failing to cross the selling level. At this point you should have sold out and again gone short. In June 1913, declined to 50, back to the same level of November 1911, and a buying point with a stop 3 points under the bottom made in February 1909, from which the last big advance started. The recovery in 1915 was rapid and Steel showed that there was good buying. When it crossed the level from 63 to 66, it was in a very strong position and indicated higher prices and the investor and trader should have bought more.

It went through the Resistance Levels of 80 to 82 in December 1915, advancing to 89 and showing that it was eventually going much higher. In January 1916, it declined to 80, getting support at the same level where previous tops had been made. In March 1916, advanced to 87. Failing to cross 89 indicated a reaction. In April 1916, again declined to 80. This was another sure buying point with a stop loss order at 77. The advance followed and Steel crossed 89 and then crossed 94⅞, the highest in history, which indicated much higher prices. In November 1916, it advanced to 129; in the panic of December 1916, declined to 101; in January 1917, rallied to 115; in February 1917, declined to 99. This was a buying level with a stop at 98, or 3 points under the low level of 1916. As long as Steel could hold above 95, the old top, it was in strong position and indicated much higher levels.

In May 1917, it advanced to 136. Here was some of the heaviest volume of trading in history and the weekly and monthly charts as well as the 3-point moves showed that Steel was making top for another decline. In December 1917, it declined to 80, the old support level and a point to buy for a rally, protected with a stop loss order at 77. In February 1918, advanced to 98; in March 1918, declined to 87. Failing to get back near the old low levels indicated higher prices. In May 1918, advanced to 113, but failed to cross the high of January 1917. In June 1918, declined to 97; August 1918, advanced to 116, where it met good selling just 3 points above the top of May 1918. The weekly chart showed it was making top and it should have been sold short. In February 1919, declined to 89, making a bottom 2 points higher than in March 1918, indicating a buying point. In July 1919, advanced to 115; failing to cross the high of August 1918 indicated that the stock should be sold short. In August 1919, had a sharp decline to 99 and in October advanced to 112, making a lower top than in July, another indication for a short sale and that the stock was going lower. In December 1919, declined to 101, making a bottom 2 points higher than the previous bottom, an indication for a rally. In January 1920, advanced to 109, making a lower top than October 1919. Notice that from May 1917, all of the tops were lower, just the same as they were in 1911 and 1912, which indicated good selling. In February 1920, Steel declined to 93, breaking the previous support levels and indicating lower prices. In April 1920, advanced to 107, again making a lower top and indicating that it was a short sale. In December 1920, declined to 77. Breaking the previous support levels at 80, which were made in 1915 and 1917, indicated lower prices. In May 1921, advanced to 86 and in June declined to 70½. At this level there was good support and the daily and weekly high and low charts showed that it was making bottom and that it should be bought for another advance.

The advance started and Steel began to make progressive tops and bottoms, working higher from each reaction until October 1923, when it advanced to 111. Failing to cross the top of October 1919 indicated at least a reaction and until it could cross these Resistance Levels, which began in May 1918, and were running right across around 109 to 116, it indicated lower prices. In November 1922, declined to 100 and in March 1923, advanced to 109. Again failing to make the last top of October 1922 indicated lower prices. In July 1923, it declined to 86; in August, rallied to 94 and in October 1923, declined to 86, the same level. Making bottoms for several months at this level showed strong support, and the stock should have been bought with a stop at 83. In February 1924, it advanced to 109, the same top as March 1922; in May 1924, declined to 95, making a higher bottom and showing better support. An advance followed and it crossed all the tops made between 1918 and 1922, an indication of much higher prices, and when it crossed 112, traders and investors should have bought more stock.

In January 1925, it advanced to 129, the same level where it made top in November 1916; in March 1925, declined to 113. This was a buying level because it was around the top levels where resistance had been met before. In November 1925, it advanced to a new high of 139. Going 3 points above the old high level of 1917 indicated higher prices to follow later. In December 1925, declined to 129 and in January 1926, advanced to 138. Failing to cross the high of November 1925, the stock should have been sold out and traders should have gone short with a stop at 142. In April 1926, it declined to 117, getting support at a higher level than in March 1925, indicating higher prices. The weekly chart at this time showed good support.

An advance followed and all high levels were crossed, and in August 1926, it advanced to 159. In October 1926, it declined to 134, getting support just under the top levels of 1925 and early 1926. Another big advance followed, and in May 1927, the old stock advanced to 176, and at the time it sold ex-dividend 40 per cent, the main trend was still up. Trading in the new stock began in December 1926, at 117 and in January 1927, it declined to 111¼. Failing to break 3 points under the last low level of March 1925, which was 113, indicated support and a buying level with a stop at 110. While the stock was slow around low levels, it showed that good accumulation was taking place and that it was getting in position to go higher again.

In May 1927, it advanced to 126 and in June 1927, declined to 119, where good support was indicated and a rally followed. When the stock crossed 126, it was the place to buy more, as it indicated higher prices, making progressive higher bottoms and higher tops. In September 1927, advanced to 160 and in October 1927, reacted to 192. Failing to get back to the old top of 126 showed good support and a buying level. The volume was very heavy at this time and the decline was quick and sharp, therefore traders should have covered shorts and bought. In December 1927, rallied to 155. Failing to reach the old top indicated another reaction to follow. In February 1928, declined to 138 and in April 1928, advanced to 154. Failing to cross the top of December indicated that it should be sold short. In June 1928, declined to 132. Failing to reach the bottom of October 1927 indicated a buying level with a stop loss order under the old bottom. The advance was resumed and in November 1928, the top was reached at 172. While this was the highest price at which the new stock had ever sold and above the top of 160 in September 1927, it was still under the high of 176, which the old stock made in May 1927. In December 1928, a decline followed to 149¾, where the stock again showed good support and the trend turned up and crossed the high of 176, which indicated high prices. In January 1929, advanced to 193; in February declined to 169; in March advanced to 193. Failing to cross the old top was an indication to sell out and go short. No doubt at this time there were heavy selling orders in this stock all the way up from 194 to 200, as selling orders always appear around these even figures. The people who set these prices failed to get out.

In March 1929, it reacted to 172 and again in April advanced to 192. Failing for the third time to cross the top of January 1929, indicated a short sale with a stop at 196. In May 1929, it declined to 162½. While this broke the previous low levels of February and March 1929, the stock did not get back near where it started in December 1928. There was good support and the weekly chart showed that the main trend had turned up. From this support level, the final grand rush followed. Steel, advancing on heavy volume, crossed the tops at 192 and 193, which was an indication for much higher prices. At no time did it close 3 consecutive days with losses, or 3 days lower, until it reached 261¾ on September 3, 1929, making the final grand rush of nearly 100 points.

Notice that this is when Steel was in its 29th year. I have stated before that stocks have their final grand rush and big advances after they have been well distributed and investors have bought them; then when the stock gets scarce it is easy to put it up, but when these final grand rushes come, the investors should sell out. If the investor had been following this advance with a stop loss order 10 points from every top, the stop loss order would not have been caught until Steel reacted from 261¾ to 251¾, when he should have sold out and gone short. In October 1929, Steel declined to 205 and in the same month rallied to 234, and in November 1929, declined to 150, getting back to the same level where it made bottom in December 1928, and the place to buy with a stop loss order at 147. In December 1929, advanced to 189 and in the same month reacted to 157, making a higher bottom and again a buying level. In February 1930, advanced to 189, the same level it made in December 1929. This was the place to sell out and go short. In February it declined to 177, again making a higher bottom from which an advance followed. Crossing 189, the tops of December 1929, and February 1930, indicated higher prices. In April 1930, advanced to 198¾, from which a reaction followed. No doubt there were heavy selling orders in around 200, because for some time previous to this the newspapers had talked about Steel making 200. Naturally, the traders who wanted to sell placed orders at the even figure, but failed to get out. Steel should get support on a reaction to around 189, but should it break the low level of February 1930, at 177, would again indicate lower prices. However, traders and investors should watch it until the weekly and monthly high and low charts show distribution and indicate that it is meeting with resistance and getting ready to go lower.

Every trader and investor should have a graph or chart, showing the swings of the stock that he is trading in, as far back as he can get them. He can then see whether it is making higher bottoms and higher tops or lower bottoms and lower tops and know the position that the stock is in. Remember that after a stock has a final grand rush, it will be a long time before it ever reaches this level again, as we have shown in the case of American Smelting & Refining and other stocks which made top in 1906 and did not cross this level again until 1926 to 1929. So the investor should avoid getting tied up with stocks after they have had the final grand rush, because they are likely to work lower for a long time to come.

WHAT TO DO WITH OLD STOCKS THAT WORK OPPOSITE THE TREND

When old or seasoned stocks start working against the trend of the general market, there is something wrong and investors and traders should get out of them and leave them alone. For example:

American Woolen - This had been a good old investment stock for many years and the Company made a large amount of money during the War days. It made low at 12 in 1914 and advanced to 169 in December 1919, where big distribution was indicated and the trend turned down. In February 1920, it declined to 114; in April rallied to 143, and in May broke 114, which showed that it was going lower; in December 1920, declined to 56. It held up well during 1921, which showed that it was getting good support and was going to have a good advance, which it did. Making bottom ahead of other stocks, it was an early leader and advanced until March 1923, when it reached 110. Notice that it failed to reach 116, the last high made in May 1920. This was a selling level where both investors and traders should have sold out. From that time on, it worked lower, never showing much rallying power and indicating that there was something wrong with the company. However, earnings for the previous years were showing up poor and it was easy to find out that the company was now badly managed, and having had heavy inventories after the War, on which there were big losses, the stock naturally felt the influence of the decreased earnings. In 1924 it broke 56, the low of 1920, which was an indication that it was going lower. It failed to rally in the Fall of 1924, when other stocks started up, and worked against the trend until 1927, when it declined to 17; then rallied in September to 28 and in June 1928, declined to 14. In November 1928, rallied to 32; then declined until October 1929, when it reached a low of 6. The Company has been showing a deficit for several years and probably has now reached the worst and the stock may be in position to work higher in the future. In February 1930, it rallied to 20 and in March 1930, declined to 13. It could be bought on reactions now, but it would be better to wait until it crosses 20, when it will indicate a better rally. However, the earnings at this time do not indicate any important bull market in American Woolen in the near future.

It is important to study what stocks do up to the time they are 10 years old; then what they do when they are 20 to 30 years old, and how they act when 40 to 50 years old.

SAFETY OF INVESTMENTS

Hoping and expecting for too much profit and taking undue risks is what causes many of the losses in Wall Street. Savings Banks are considered the safest way of investing your money. You receive 4 to 4½ per cent on your account. The next safest investments are good bonds and first mortgages, which return about 6 per cent on your money. When you go beyond this in investments and buy stocks or bonds that pay more than 6 per cent, you have crossed the danger line and departed from the rule of safety. It is better to select good stocks which pay smaller dividends and buy them at the right time than it is to buy bonds which pay high rates and are dangerous. If bonds have to be sold to yield more than 6 per cent, there is something wrong with them. You can often select a stock that is paying a dividend of 4 per cent, which has future possibilities and will later pay 8 or 10 per cent dividends, and your investment will return a big profit because your stock will advance in price. Bonds very seldom advance very much and often go below the price which you pay for them, causing a shrinkage in your invested capital. Even the very best bonds decline under unfavorable conditions. British Consols and United States Bonds have had big declines in time of war. This shows you that it is necessary to keep a chart on bonds or a group of bonds and watch for a change in trend just the same as you watch for change in trend in active stocks. The time comes when you must sell out bonds which are starting to decline and get into better and safer bonds or wait for another opportunity.

By studying the action of the bond market and bond prices, you will be able to determine what the stock market is going to do later and what general business is going to do. Bond prices in 1928 gave the indication of a decline in stock prices to follow and of a business depression.

CHAPTER VII
HOW TO SELECT THE EARLY AND LATE LEADERS

In every bull campaign there are always stocks that lead in the first section of the campaign. Some of them make top in the early stages of the campaign and never go higher, then work lower, while other stocks are going up. In the next section of a bull campaign, new leaders are taken up and they make top and do not lead in the third section of the bull campaign, when other new leaders are again taken up. Finally in the fourth or last section of a bull campaign the late leaders are brought into line and have big advances.

In every group of stocks there are always some that are in a weak position and some that are in a strong position, working opposite to the general trend. Therefore, it is necessary to determine the stocks which are in strong position and will become leaders, and those in weak position which will continue to work lower or will be leaders in a bear market. In the 1921 to 1929 Bull Campaign only a limited few were active and continued to lead each year. Some stocks finished and made top in 1922, others made top in 1923, 1925, 1926, 1927, and a majority of the list made top in 1928. In November 1928, the averages of all stocks traded in on the New York Stock Exchange reached the highest price in the campaign. Yet, the Dow-Jones 30 Industrials reached a record high on September 3, 1929, and many stocks which were late leaders had big advances in the Spring and Summer of 1929. The time to make money trading in stocks is when they are leading, either up or down. Therefore, it is necessary to study each individual stock in a group of stocks in order to determine its position.

CHEMICAL STOCKS

When I wrote TRUTH OF THE STOCK TAPE in January 1923, I said that the Chemical and Airplane stocks would be the leaders in the next bull market. Therefore, it was necessary to analyze the different chemical stocks to determine which ones would be the best to buy in the different stages of the bull campaign.

American Agricultural Chemical - In April, May, June and July 1919, this stock reached extreme high and distribution took place. It declined until August 1921, reaching a low of 27; then in August 1922, made a high of 42. In April 1923, it again declined to 27, the low of 1921. This was not a sign of strength because if it was going to work higher, it should have made a higher bottom and the rally in 1922 was small compared with other stocks. The trend continued down, the stock being very weak during 1924, and in June it reached a low of 7, which was the lowest level since 1907, when the low was 10. This showed that the stock was in a very weak position and was not one of the Chemical stocks to buy for a big advance. In January 1926, high was 34. While this was above the top of 1923, it failed to reach the high of 1922, the first year of the bull campaign. The trend again turned down and in April 1927, it declined to 8, holding one point above the low of June 1922. This was a buying level, for a rally, protected with a stop at 6. Low-priced stocks of this kind should be protected with stop loss orders about one point under a previous low level. A slow rally followed and in November 1928, a high of 26 was recorded. Note this top was below 1926 top, showing that the stock was lowering its tops on every rally and that the main trend was down. From this top it continued down and was very weak, reaching final low in November 1929, when it sold at 4, the lowest price for over 20 years.

One of my rules is that a stock must cross its high level made in the first year of the bull campaign in order to show that it is going to be a leader in a later section of the bull campaign. The fact that American Agricultural Chemical never crossed the high of 1922 was an indication that it would not be a leader. Therefore, you should not have bought it but should have looked for a chemical stock which showed itself to be in a stronger position.

Davison Chemical - In March 1921, the low was 23. It showed good support and the advance started. In April 1922, it reached a high of 65. Here there was good selling and the trend turned down. In May 1923, low was 21.This was a buying level, that is, you should have bought around 23 to 22, protected with a stop at 20 or 3 points under the 1921 low level. Previous to the decline in May 1923, this stock had rallied to 37 in March. In August 1923, it crossed 37, the high in the early part of the year, which turned the trend up and indicated higher prices. If you had bought stock around the low level, when it crossed 38, you should have bought more and followed up with a stop loss order. In the latter part of 1923 there was a fast advance and this stock was rushed up by pools.
There was a lot of newspaper talk about it; tips were wild that it was going to several hundred dollars a share and some wild-eyed enthusiastic market letter writers said that there was a possibility of it going to $1000 a share because of the great profits to be derived from the Silica Gel process. In December 1923, the stock sold at 81. This was a sharp top on heavy volume of trading and a quick, sharp decline followed, the price working lower until April 1924, when it sold at 41. From this level it slowly advanced until July 1924, when it again sold at 61. This was another sharp advance, and a sharp decline followed. After it made a lower top in July 1924, and broke the bottom at 41 made in April 1924, it showed a weak position and indicated lower prices. In April 1925, it declined to 28, which was 5 to 7 points above the lows of 1921 and 1923. Receiving support at a higher level indicated a rally at least. In August 1925, it rallied to 46; had a reaction and again in February 1926, made a high of 46. Now, failing to cross this high level was an indication for lower prices and the stock should have been sold out and sold short with a stop at 49.

A decline followed and in March, 1927, it declined to 27, one point under the low of 1925. This was again a buying point protected with a stop at 25, or 3 points under the low of 1925. There was again good support and in July 1927, it rallied to 43. Failing to make the tops of 1925 and 1926, was a sign of weakness and indicated another decline to follow and also indicated that this stock would not be a leader in the near future. In October 1926, it declined to 23, breaking all low levels except the lows of 1921 and 1923. Here it again received support and you could have bought, protected with a stop at 20. The fact that it held at this time 2 points above the 1923 low and at the same low of 1921, showed that somebody was buying the stock around this level. It held for 6 months in a narrow, trading range, then the trend turned up. It advanced to 48 in December 1927, crossing the tops of 1925, 1926, and 1927. This was a strong indication for higher prices and indicated that the stock should be bought again on any reaction. In February 1928, it reacted to 35, where it again received good support and in April 1928, crossed 48. This was another place to buy more and the advance continued until November 1928, when the stock sold at 68, crossing all previous tops except the extreme high which was made in December 1923. There was a reaction from 68 to 54 in December 1928. In January 1929, it advanced to 69, only getting one point higher than the previous top. This was a bad sign and indicated that the stock should be sold out and sold short. It held in a narrow, trading range for some time, and in February and March made the high level; then in the latter part of March declined to 49.

Breaking back 20 points from the high level after making a double top, was a bad indication. In April 1929, it rallied to 59, again making a lower top. In May it declined to 43, making a lower bottom, still showing the trend down. In July 1929, it rallied to 56, again making a lower top, and in August declined to 46, making a slightly higher bottom than the previous low. It rallied again in the early part of October to 56. Making the same top again was an indication for a short sale.

A wide-open break followed and in the latter part of October it declined again to 21, the low level of 1923. The fact that it was supported in 1921, 1923, and 1926 around these levels was an indication to buy in 1929 at this level with a stop at 20, which would not have been caught. This proves my rule to buy with a stop loss order 3 points under the first extreme low level. For example: In March 1921, the extreme low was 23 and a stop loss order at 20 would have held every time it was bought during this period of years.

You might ask why the stock got support at this level every time. The reason was that there was some pool or some people on the inside who knew that it was worth $20 a share and every time it declined to around 25 to 21 they would buy and then sell out when it reached a level which they thought as high enough. From the low level of 21 in 1929, the stock rallied to 42 in March 1930. Should this stock hold for a few years and not break back to the low of 1929 on the next decline, it may be a future leader. You can see that this stock was an early leader in the 1921 to 1929 Bull Campaign, making high in December 1923, and never getting higher during the following 6 years, while other chemical stocks in strong position made higher each year following.

Air Reduction - Made low at 30 in 1920, and again in June 1921, made this same low, a double bottom, which was a good indication for a big advance to follow. In March 1923, it advanced to 72, showing that it was an early leader. It declined to 56 in June 1923. In January 1924, it made a new high at 81 and in February 1925, advanced to 112, the highest in its history. It made higher bottoms and higher tops in 1926, 1927, and 1928, showing at all times that it was a leader because it was making higher bottoms while other stocks, like American Agricultural Chemical and Davison Chemical, worked lower from every top instead of making new tops. Air Reduction was a late mover and a fast mover in the last final grand rush in the 1929 Bull Campaign. It reached. final high in October 1929, selling at 223. It made a sharp top, was very active at the top, fluctuating over a wide range, with a very large volume of sales. It declined to 77 in November 1929. If you were watching this stock in August 1929, for a sign of top, these indications would show that it was nearing the end. August 1929, high 217, September 1929, high 219, only 2 points above the previous top. A sharp reaction followed and the final grand rush in October carried the stock to 223, only 6 points above the high of August and 4 points above the high of September. At the time the final high was made, nearly all other stocks had turned the main trend down. It was only natural to expect that this stock would have to follow the decline when it was so severe in other stocks.

A weekly high and low chart from August 24 to November 16, 1929, shows the top and big distribution. During the week ending October 5 , 1929, Air Reduction declined to 186 from the top of 219; then advanced to 223 during the week ending October 19. The following week it broke below 186, the bottom made during the week ending October 5. This turned the main trend down, and if you were already short, you should have sold more when it broke 186, and you could have made 100 points or more from this level in a few weeks. While this stock was a leader during the bull campaign and a late mover, finishing last, at the same time it had a decline proportionate or greater than many other stocks in the first panicky decline.

Allied Chemical - This was one of the best leaders among the chemical stocks and one of the best to buy, showing up trend most all of the time. In August 1921, the low was 34. It advanced to 91 in September 1922 ; declined to 60 in August 1923 ; and had many months of accumulation. In March 1925, it made a new high of 93. Getting above the 1922 high showed that it would be a purchase on any reaction for much higher prices later. During 1926, 1927, 1928 and 1929, it made higher bottoms and higher tops until the final top was reached in August 1929, when it sold at 255. The weekly high and low chart showed down trend at 235. The stock declined to 197 on November 13, 1929. Having a much smaller break than Air Reduction and other chemical stocks, showed that it was in a stronger position and could have a better rally when the trend turned up. It received good support and rallied to 192 in March 1930. From the above analysis you can see how Air Reduction and Allied Chemical were in strong position, while American Agricultural Chemical and Davison Chemical were in a weak position.

Dupont - Made low levels in 1922 and 1923; then made a higher bottom in 1924 and worked higher every year until September 1929, when it sold at 231. This was one of the late leaders among the chemicals. In November 1929, it declined to 80. Note how much greater decline this stock had than Allied Chemical. The reason that Dupont had so much greater decline than Allied Chemical was that Dupont had been split up and the stock distributed, while Allied Chemical had not been split up and had not declared a stock dividend. Dupont rallied to 134 in March 1930.

U. S. Industrial Alcohol - This stock was analyzed in TRUTH OF THE STOCK TAPE and its position shown to be weak because it was a late mover in the Bear Campaign of 1921 and did not make bottom until November 1921, when it sold at a low of 35. Therefore, it could be expected to be a late mover in a bull campaign later. In March, 1923, U. S. Industrial Alcohol sold as high as 73; then declined in June 1923, to 40; and in July 1924, advanced to 83, getting 10 points above the high of 1923. From this level it worked lower until May 1924, when it declined to 62. Then a sharp advance followed, reaching high at 98 in October 1925. This was the old support level on the way down. (Notice the chart shown in TRUTH OF THE STOCK TAPE.) The old support level became a Resistance Level and a selling level when the stock rallied to this price. It showed weakness and worked lower until March 1926, when it reached 45, holding 5 points above the low of 1923 and 10 points above the low of 1921. This was again a buying level. In February 1927, it advanced to 89, failing to reach the top of 1925. In March 1927, it declined to 69 where there was good support and the trend turned up again. In December 1927, it crossed 98. This was an indication for higher prices and you should have bought more. In March 1928, it made high at 122. Here there was good selling and in June 1928, it declined to 102. Holding above the old top level of 98 and failing to break 100, was an indication of higher prices later. After that the stock gradually worked higher and in August 1929, the final grand rush started when the stock started up from 175 and advanced to 243 in October 1929. It then declined to 95 in November 1929, getting 5 points under the low of 1928, but back to the old support level around 95 to 98, which had been Resistance Levels for years both on the down side and on the up side before they were crossed. After the bottom was reached in November 1929, there was a sharp, quick rally to 155 in December, when the trend again turned down. In March 1930, it broke back to 100, showing the stock to be in a weak position.

It is very important to note the old tops of this stock in 1916, 1917, and 1918, which were from 167 to 169. When these tops were crossed it indicated much higher prices and instead of selling short, you could have made big money buying it at this high level. Note the support levels at 95 to 98 in 1916, 1917, and 1918, and 1919, and again in 1929 the bottom at 95.

A daily high and low chart on U. S. Industrial Alcohol for September and October 1929, is very important and will show you its position very clearly. On September 3, 1929, the day average top was made on the Dow-Jones Industrial Stocks, U. S. Industrial Alcohol sold at 213½; declined to 200 on September 5; rallied to 212 on September 9 and 10; declined again on September 10 and 11 to 200, the same low as September 5. Then, when it broke 3 points under this level, or sold at 197, you should go short. On September 12 it advanced to 210½; September 13 declined to 198½, only 1½ points under the previous bottom; September 20 had a fast run-up to a new high of 226½; September 25 declined to 204½, still holding above the previous low level; September 27 high 220; October 4 low, 201, a higher bottom than September 5, 9, and 10, and still higher than September 13. This was a sure indication to go short if it declined to 197, but as long as it was making higher bottoms, it was good to buy with a stop at this price, or with a stop at 100. On October 11, 1929, final top was reached at 243½. From October 4 to 11, the stock closed every day with a gain and on October 11 closed 3½ points over October 10. Then on October 14 opened one point higher and closed at 233, the low of the day, down 8 points.

This was an indication on the daily chart to go short. A wide-open break followed and you should have sold more short when it broke 200, or at 197 stop. On November 13 it declined to 95 and on December 9 rallied to 155 and started down again, declined to 98½ in March 1930. The fact that this stock could never rally above the high of December 9, 1929, and all the time was making lower bottoms on the daily and weekly charts, showed that it was in a weak position. When stocks are very active and reach high or low levels, it is always important to watch the weekly charts for a change in trend, but watch the daily charts for the first indication of change in trend. The daily chart will show you where there are Resistance Levels more clearly than the weekly chart. U. S. Industrial Alcohol was late in making bottom in the 1921 Bear Campaign and was one of the last to make top in the 1929 Bull Campaign. Watch these early and late movers and never buck the trend; do not buy them when they still show down trend or sell them short as long as they show up trend, even if they are running against the general list of leaders.

COPPER AND METAL STOCKS

Most of the copper stocks were very slow and were late leaders in the 1921 to 1929 Bull Campaign. In order to determine the best ones to trade in and those that would be early and late movers, it would be necessary for you to keep up charts and study each individual stock in the group.

American Smelting & Refining - It is well to know the history of this stock, which was a leader in the 1921 to 1929 Bull Campaign, especially from 1924 on. The high was reached in 1906 when the stock sold at 174, and the high in the 1916 Bull Campaign was 123. It declined in 1921 to 30. This was the same low as the stock s old in 1899, a very important support level. In 1925, the stock crossed 123, the high of 1916, which indicated much higher prices. It continued to make higher bottoms and higher tops, and in September 1927, crossed 174, the highest in history. There was a quick reaction to 158 in October 1927. When a stock goes into a new high level after many years, it is always a sign of higher prices but often a reaction occurs before the big advance takes place, and the time to buy is on the first or second reaction after it goes into new high territory. If you had bought American Smelting the second time it went through 174, you would have made big profits and could have pyramided on the way up.

In January 1929, American Smelting sold at 295. Then a stock dividend was declared and the stock split up on a basis of 3 new shares for one old share. The low on the new stock was 85, high 130, in September 1929, which would equal 390. It declined to 62 in November, 1929, which was a buying level. Note bottoms and support level from 58 to 61 in 1924. From low of 62, a rally followed to 79 in December 1929. After that it held in a narrow trading range, and up to this writing, March 1930, has failed to advance again to the high of December 1929.

Anaconda Copper - This stock was a late mover in the bull market of 1916, in fact, one of the last to have a fast run-up. This is one of the old copper companies and it is important to have a record of its prices a long ways back. The low in 1903 and 1904 was 15; low in the 1907 panic 25; again in 1915 and 1916 low 25. The high in November 1916, was 105, the low in 1920 was 31 and the low in 1921 was 29, getting support around the same price in 1920 and 1921 and holding 5 to 6 points above the support level of 1907, 1915 and 1916. This was a good place to buy Anaconda with a short stop, although it was slow and required patience for a long time. In 1922, high was 57 in May and September. Then it declined again to a low of 29 in May 1924, getting support again for the third time, which was a sure indication for higher prices later, provided it did not break 26, or 3 points under the support level. In May 1924, it worked up slowly, making higher bottoms and higher tops each year, but remained in a sideways movement, showing accumulation, and did not cross 57, the high of 1922, until December 1927, when it advanced to 60 and never reacted to 53 again. When the stock crossed the tops of six years past, it was safer to buy at new high levels for a bigger advance than it had been before, because crossing all of these old tops was a sign of a fast move up and a big one.

In November, 1928, it crossed 105, the highest price in its history. This was another place to buy the stock for higher prices. In March 1929, it advanced to 174. A stock dividend was declared and the new stock sold at 140 in March 1929; declined to 99 in May, rallied to 134 in September, making a top 6 points lower than the highest point reached in March 1929, which showed that distribution was taking place and the stock should be sold short after it had made a lower top. It declined rapidly after breaking 125, with very small rallies; broke 99 and on December 23, 1929, declined to 68. A feeble rally followed, and the stock reached 80 in February 1930.

Kennecott Copper - This stock was an early leader in the 1921 to 1929 Bull Campaign and advanced ahead of every stock in the copper group. Therefore, it was one of the good copper stocks to buy. The low in 1920 was 15 and it failed to get as low in 1921, making a higher bottom and a higher top each year until 1927, when a runaway move started from around 65. It advanced to 165, reaching final top in February 1929. A stock dividend was declared and the new stock made high in March 1929, when it sold at 104. It declined to 50 in November 1929. This was the same low reached in March 1926, from which the stock started up. This stock showed plainly in 1921 and 1922 that it was going to be a leader. The fact that it failed to break the low of 1920, making a higher bottom in 1921, showed that it was in position to lead and you should have bought it in preference to Anaconda or some of the other stocks.

It is always important to watch stocks and buy them after they cross the zone of accumulation or sell them after they break under the zone of distribution. By doing this, you will get quick profits without wearing out your patience and getting caught in a sideways movement.

84

International Nickel - This stock was a late mover in the 1921 to 1929 Bull Campaign. It accumulated for a long time, but if you waited to buy until it crossed the zone of accumulation, you would have made quick money and saved time by not getting in too soon. The 1920 high was 26, low 12; 1921 high 17, low 12; 1922 high 19, low 12; 1923 high 16, low 11; 1924 high 27, low 11½. You can see that during all these years the stock was receiving support around 11 to 12. Somebody was taking all there was offered. Therefore, it was safe to buy with a stop at 10, or, say, 3 points under 12, which would make the stop at 9. In 1922, the first year of the Bull Campaign, high was 19. My rule says that it is always better to wait until the stock advances above the first year of the Bull Campaign. In November 1924, the stock crossed 20, which was above the high of 1922, a sure sign for higher prices. This was the place to buy. In September 1925, it made 25, 3 points above the high of 1920. This was the point to buy more. In November and December 1925, it advanced to 48. The weekly chart showed top and temporary period of distribution. In March 1926, it declined to 33 and made the same bottom again in May. You should have bought it with a stop loss order at 30, or 3 points under the old bottom. It started up and made higher bottoms each month and in April 1927, crossed 48. This was another place to buy more. It continued to work higher, making higher bottoms and higher tops; crossed 227, the old top of 1915 and 1916, and advanced to 325 in January 1929, when a stock dividend was declared.

The new stock was traded in on the New York Curb and made a low of 32 in November 1928, the same low as was made in March and May 1926, from which the big trend turned up. After a stock is split up it is always important to watch the old high or low levels from which previous moves started in the old stock, as the new stock will often receive support and meet selling at these same levels. Therefore, when the new stock of International Nickel declined to 32, it was worth buying with a stop at 29. The new stock advanced and made a high of 73 in January 1929. Distribution took place around this level and it declined to 25 in November 1929; then rallied to 42 in March 1930.

The fact that International Nickel held at the same bottom around 12 for five consecutive years, from 1920 to 1924, showed big accumulation, and indicated that the trading was for some big buyer who did not bid for the stock, but who took all that was offered. While the stock was a late mover in the 1924 to 1929 Bull Campaign, it made the greatest advance of any stock in the metal group, going up 313 points from the low of 1924. It shows the value of buying stocks after they have had big accumulation over a long period of time and of buying them after they get out of the zone of accumulation. The big move in this stock really started in April 1927, at 41 and in 21 months to January 1929, the stock had advanced 280 points, or an average gain of over 13 points per month. The greatest reaction at any time was 25 points and this was from 99 to 74. After it crossed 105 in April 1928, there was a wild runaway bull move. Make up a weekly high and low chart on this stock, especially on the new stock from November 1928, to date, and you will see the sharp top at 73 made in the week ending January 26, 1929. A sharp decline followed to 57; then a rally to 67, followed by a sideways distribution and a decline to 40½ in March 1929. From this bottom it rallied to 60½ in the week ending September 21. From this third lower top a panicky decline followed. The stock sold at 25 in November 1929, and rallied to 42 in March 1930.

EQUIPMENT STOCKS

The stocks in any group that make bottom first, make top earlier in a Bull Campaign.

American Brake Shoe & Foundry - This stock made low in December 1920, when it sold at 40. It accumulated during 1921 and was a leader in 1922. The fact that it did not sell lower in 1921 than it did in 1920 showed that it was getting ready to lead in the next bull market. It reacted and accumulated in 1923 and 1924 and was again a leader in 1925 and reached high in February 1926, at 280. In May 1926, declined to 110 and in March 1927, rallied to 152, when a stock dividend was declared. After that there were not any big trading opportunities in it.

American Car & Foundry - This was another stock that made low in December 1920, at 111 and was a leader in 1922. In October 1922, it sold at 200; reacted and accumulated in 1923 and 1924 and advanced to 232 in March 1925, when a stock dividend was declared. It never had any big move during the balance of the 1921 to 1929 Bull Campaign. Showed distribution and down trend from September 1925, to November 1929, when the new stock sold at 76.

American Locomotive - This stock was an early leader and made 145 in 1923; a stock dividend was declared and the new stock accumulated between 65 and 76. A fast advance started from 84 in December 1924, and reached top in March 1925, at 144. It failed to cross the old top of 145 made in 1923. After the trend turned down, this stock continued to work lower while other stocks were advancing, until June 1928, when it declined to 87. Then it advanced to 136 in July 1929, and declined to go in November 1929.

Baldwin Locomotive - This has always been one of the good, fast movers because the supply of stock has always been very small. The total number of floating shares was seldom over 100,000. In June 1921, the low was 63, only 2 points under the 1919 low, and if you had bought at the 1919 low with a stop 2 points lower, the stop would not have been caught. It was a bull leader in 1922 and reached 144 in March 1923. In May 1924, it declined to 105 and in February 1925, advanced to 146, getting 2 points above the top of March 1923. It was a short sale at this level protected with a stop 2 points over the old top. In March 1925, it declined to 107, getting support 2 points higher than May 1924. This was another buying point. In February 1926, it advanced to 136 and in March 1926, when the market had a big panicky decline, it reached 93, the same low level of December 1921, and January 1923, from which a big advance started. After the decline in March 1926, the trend again turned up and the stock met selling around 124 to 126 from July to October 1926, and in November crossed 128 and went right on through 144 and 146, the tops of 1923 and 1925. Later it crossed 156, the highest rice made in its history. Making a new high for all time indicated a further big advance and you should have bought more and pyramided all the way up.

The stock reached the extreme high of 285 in March 1928; had a quick decline. Then a stock dividend was declared, and the old stock was exchanged on a basis of 4 new shares for one of the old. The new stock sold at 66½ in August 1929; then turned the main trend down, as you can see by making up a weekly high and low chart. Baldwin declined to 15 on October 29, 1929, equal to 60 for the old stock, which was 3 points under the low of June 1921. Then followed a rally to 38 in February 1930. This shows you that when American Brake Shoe, American Car & Foundry and American Locomotive were on the down trend, Baldwin was on the up trend and made top later in the Bull Campaign, while the others made top in the early years of the bull market and never went higher. The chart showed that Baldwin was in stronger position.

Westinghouse Electric - A yearly high and low chart from 1901 to date indicates August 1921, low 39; February 1923, high 67; May, June and July 1923, same low at 53, where it received strong support; and in January 1924, advanced to 65. In May 1924, it declined to 56, receiving support at a higher level than the previous bottom. In December 1924, it crossed 67 the high of 1923 and advanced to 84 in January 1925; declined to 66 in March; rallied to 79 in August and again in February 1926, made the same top at 79. In May 1926, it declined to 65, only one point under the low made in 1923. This was a buying level with a stop at 63. See monthly chart 1925-1927. In August 1927, it crossed 84, the high of 1925 and later crossed 92, the tops of 1904, 1905 and 1906, which was a sure sign of much higher prices. In November 1928, it crossed 116, the highest price in its history, which was made in 1902. Making a new high record after so many years of accumulation was a sure sign of a big advance to follow.

This stock was in the same position as Baldwin when it crossed 156 and in the same position as American Smelting when it crossed 174 after so many years. After Westinghouse crossed 116, it never reacted to 112 until it advanced to 292 in August 1929. The last advance of 100 points was made in 6 weeks. This is another example of my rule of fast moves of 6 to 7 weeks in the final grand rush. Refer to weekly charts from January 5, 1929, to April 12, 1930.. The stock made a sharp top; declined to 275; rallied to 289, making a lower top; then broke 275, the bottom of the first reaction, which showed that the trend had turned down. A fast decline followed, reaching 202 on October 3; a quick rally followed to October 11, when it advanced to 244. Then started on another panicky decline. When it broke 200, you should have sold more stock and pyramided on the way down. On October 29 it sold at 100; then rallied to 154; declined to 103 on November 13, making a higher bottom. This was an indication of a strong position and you should have bought with a stop under 100. The advance started and the stock reached 159; then declined again to 125 and started up. The last tops on the weekly chart were at 154 and 159 and when it crossed 160 was an indication for a much further advance and you should have bought more stock. It advanced to 195 in March 1930; met good selling and then reacted.

FOOD STOCKS

Beech-Nut Packing - July 1922, low 10, March 1923, high 84, It held in a slow, narrow, trading range until April 1927, when it reached a low of 50; then advanced to 101 in January 1929; declined to 45 in November, the same low as it made in April 1924. This was a buying level for a rally.

California Packing - July 1921, low 54; advanced in 1922; held up well in 1923; then advanced rapidly in 1924 and 1925; reached top in February 1926, at 179; had a sham decline to 121 in March 1926. Later declared 100 per cent stock dividend and had no more big moves the balance of the 1921 to 1929 Bull Campaign.

Continental Baking "A" - Reached high in 1925 when it sold at 144; then worked lower to April 1928, when it sold as low as 27. In July 1929, it rallied to go and in October 1929, declined to 25, holding 2 points above the low level of 1928, a support level, where you should have bought with a stop loss order at 24.

Corn Products - This stock was reviewed in TRUTH OF THE STOCK TAPE. It made high in 1924 when it reached 187 and a stock dividend was declared, and an exchange made on a basis of 5 new for one old share. The new stock held in a narrow, trading range during 1924, 1925 and 1926 where it was accumulated. It became more active in 1927 and advanced to 126 in October 1929; declined to 70 in November 1929; then rallied to 109 in April 1930.

Cuyamel Fruit - This stock was an early mover and also a late mover in the 1921 to 1929 Bull Campaign. In January 1924, it made top at 74; then worked lower until February, March and April 1927, when it declined to 30. At this level it was accumulated and started up again; reached top in the early part of October 1929, when it sold at 126; then declined to 85 on October 29, 1929.

General Foods - Postum Cereal was an early mover and made its first top in February 1923, when it sold at 134. Later a stock dividend of 100 per cent was declared and accumulation of the new stock took place around 47 to 58. It crossed the Resistance Level at 58 to 60 in September 1924, and advanced to 143 in August 1925, when there was another stock dividend. The new stock declined to 65 in November 1925, and in May 1928, advanced to 136. It was later consolidated with General Foods, which was distributed in 1929, and reached top at 81 in April 1929; then declined to 35 in October, 1929. This company is controlled by the Morgan interests and no doubt in later years will advance to much higher prices. You should keep a chart on it, watch it and buy it at the right time.

Ward Baking "B" - In April 1924, made low at 14, where it showed big accumulation and good support. In October 1925, advanced to 95. The trend then turned down and it worked lower to October 1929, when it sold at 2. It made lower bottoms and lower tops in 1926, 1927, 1928 and 1929. It was a short sale all the time while some of the other stocks in the same group showed up trend. This was one of the new stocks, organized in recent years and was overcapitalized, which caused the big decline after it had been distributed to the public.

MOTORS OR AUTOMOBILE STOCKS

This group of stocks furnished some of the best leaders during the 1921 to 1929 Bull Campaign and traders who studied each individual stock were able to determine the stocks which were in position to have the biggest advances.

Chrysler - Formerly Maxwell Motors, was one of the early movers and leaders in the 1921 to 1929 Bull Campaign. The Maxwell "A" stock sold at 38 in 1921; advanced to 75 in 1922; declined to 36 in 1923. Failing to go 3 points under the 1921 low level showed good support and was the place to buy. The advance started after the name was changed to Chrysler. The first big advance culminated in November 1925, when it sold at 253. At this time a stock dividend was declared and the new stock sold at 56 in December 1925. In March 1926, it declined to 29; showed good accumulation and started up, making higher bottoms and higher tops during 1926 and 1927. After meeting good selling around 60 to 63 from August 1927, to March 1928, the big move started and in October 1928, the stock reached top at 140, where big distribution took place, lasting about 4 months. Then the main trend turned down, as you can see from the monthly and weekly charts, and this stock was in a real bear market from January 1929, on.

It declined to 66 in May 1929; rallied to 79. It showed great weakness and a lot of stock was distributed between 66 and 78. In September, 1929, it broke 66, the old bottom, and declined to 26 in November 1929, which was 2½ points under the low of March 1926.

Then a rally followed to April 1930, when it sold at 42. This stock was a public favorite and was distributed at very high levels; that is the reason it declined to such a low level and had such a feeble rally up to this writing.

Hudson Motors - Was a late mover in the 1921 to 1929 Bull Campaign. May 1922, low 19; August, September and October 1922, low 20. March 1924, high 29. May 1924, low 21. Thus you will see that the extreme low was made in 1922, and the bottom in 1923 was one point higher and again in 1924 made bottom one point higher. The stock held in a narrow, trading range for 3 years while accumulation was taking place. In December 1924, it crossed 32, the high of 1922, and a fast advance followed. In November 1925, first top was made at 139. In December a sharp decline followed, carrying the price down to 96. Then it rallied to 123, where distribution took place during January, February, and March 1926. The main trend turned down and the price worked lower until October 1926, when it sold at 44. Accumulation again took place and the stock started up. In March 1928, it reached top at 99. After that it held in a range between 77 and 97 until September 1929. This showed another period of big distribution. In November 1929, the stock declined to 38, not quite 3 points under the low of October 1926. This, being an old Resistance Level, was a buying point. The stock rallied to 62 in January 1930.

General Motors - This stock has made more millionaires and more paupers than any other stock in the motor group. Instead of its abbreviation being GMO it should be G.O.M., meaning "Grand Old Man" of the motor industry. It holds the record for being a bull Leader in the 1915 and 1916, 1918 and 1919 Bull Campaigns, and had some of its greatest advances in the 1924 to 1929 Bull Campaign. (See yearly charts, 1911-1930.)

The low in 1913 was 24 and the top in November 1916, was 850. Then a stock dividend was declared and the stock split up. It declined to 75 in November 1917, where it received good support and showed big accumulation. It led the 1919 Bull Campaign; reached top in November when it sold at 400. A quick decline followed to 225 in February 1920; then rallied to 410 in March 1920, when the stock was split up on a basis of 10 for 1. In March 1920, the new stock sold at 42, which was equal to 420 on the basis of the old stock. There was big distribution and the trend turned down and did not reach bottom until January and March 1922, when it sold at 8¼, which was equal to 82½ compared with 420 top in March 1920. At this time there were about 50 million shares of stock outstanding. It moved in a very slow range, finally reaching 17 in April and May 1922; declined to 13 in July 1923; rallied to 16 in August, and in January 1924, sold at 16, the same top. In April and May 1924, declined to 13 again, making the same bottom. It held in a trading range between 8¼ and 16 from October 1920, to June 1924. A period of 3½ years of accumulation certainly meant that a big advance would follow later and that it would last a long time before it reached the period for distribution.

In June 1924, there was an exchange of stock on a basis of 4 shares of new stock for 10 of the old, which reduced the number of shares outstanding. The new stock started up from 52 and worked higher until early November 1925, when top was reached at 149 for a temporary reaction. A quick decline followed and the stock sold at 106 in the latter part of November. The upward trend was again resumed, while White Motors and other motor stocks were moving down, just opposite to General Motors. In August 1926, another top was made at 225 and a stock dividend of 50 per cent was declared. The new stock declined to 141 in September 1926; then advanced to 173 in October, where a temporary top was made and a sharp decline followed in November, making a low of 137⅝, just about 3 points under the low of September, where there was large volume and good support, and after a period of accumulation the trend turned up again. In March 1927, the price crossed 173, the high of October 1926, and the big upswing was again on. Top was reached in October 1927, when General Motors sold at 282. There was a stock dividend of 100 per cent declared in August 1927. Trading in the new stock, when issued, started on the New York Curb. It sold at 111 in August and then started up and in October 1927, sold at 141, equal to 283 for the old stock. It declined to 125 in November and December, where it received support and started to work higher. In March 1928, crossed 141, the high of October 1927, and a rapid advance followed. In May 1928, General Motors made top at 210; a sharp decline started and in June it sold at 169, where support was again encountered and the advance resumed. In October and November 1928, top was again reached at 225. Note this is the same level as top in 1926. There was heavy selling around this level and big distribution took place.

A decline in December carried the stock down to 182, when another stock dividend was declared. In December 1928, the new stock declined to 74, and then slowly worked up until March 1929, when top was reached at 191¾. At this time the volume of sales was over 1½ million shares per week for 4 consecutive weeks, showing big distribution. On March 26, the day of the big decline, General Motors sold at 77¼ and in the latter part of April rallied to 88½ with the weekly volume of sales over one million shares, showing good selling. The fact that it failed to reach the old top was a sign to sell short. The decline started and in May the low level of March was broken, a sure sign of a down trend. In the latter part of July, General Motors sold at 66¼ and on September 3, 1929, rallied to 79¼, the last top, with a weekly volume of 1½ million shares. This indicated good selling, especially as the stock failed to get 3 points above the top made at 77¼ on July 3. There were 4 weeks' bottoms around 71¼ to 72¼ made between August 21 and September 21. During the week ending September 28 General Motors broke 72 and declined to 66. When it broke 72 it was time to sell more short and pyramid on the way down. On October 29 it sold at 33½ and the sales for the day were 971,300 shares and the sales for the week were 2,225,600 and for the next 3 weeks sales ran over one million shares per week. On October 31, 1929, the stock rallied to 46½; then declined to 36 on November 7. Sales for the week ending November 16 were 923,000 shares. For the week ending November 23 the sales were only 318,000 shares and the stock rallied, showing liquidation had run its course. On December 9 and 10 it rallied to 44½; on January 18, 1930, declined to 37½, sales 320,000 shares, which indicated no heavy liquidation. This was a second higher bottom after the stock crossed 42, where it had met resistance for several weeks, and again indicated higher prices. On April 9, 1930, General Motors advanced to 54, the volume of sales increasing.

It is important to note that from June 1924, to March 1929, no reaction lasted more than one month, or that when a reaction ran into the second month, the price did not decline 3 points under the low of the previous month. This is a good rule to follow - never sell a stock short that will not react more than one month from a top. During the time that General Motors reacted only one month and then went higher, Hudson, Mack, White and other motor stocks, which advanced in 1924 and 1925 when General Motors was accumulating, were going down and showed weak positions, while General Motors showed a strong up trend. General Motors, having been a leader in all of the bull campaigns from 1914 to 1929, you cannot expect it to be a leader in the next bull campaign, so look over your motor stock group and pick a leader that shows accumulation and indicates it is in a position to lead.

Mack Trucks - This was another early mover among the motor stocks. One of the reasons for this was the small capitalization. There were only 339,000 shares outstanding and it was easy for a pool to move this stock up. The low was 25 in 1921, and in April 1923, the high was 94. In June 1923, low was 64, where it had big accumulation during 1923 and 1924. This showed that somebody was buying all of the stock they could get, preparing for another big upward move. In August 1924, the stock crossed 94, the high of 1923; made top at 242 in November 1925, where distribution took place and a stock dividend declared. Then the main trend turned down. In March 1926, it declined to 104; rallied to 136 in August 1926. After that made lower tops and lower bottoms - January 1927, low 89; May 1927, high 118; April 1928, low 83; February and March 1929, high 114, a lower top than May 1927; March and May 1929, declined to 91; September 1929, rallied to 104. This was a very feeble rally and showed that big distribution was taking place. The distribution period really lasted from 1925 to 1929. The stock declined to 55 in November 1929. Note last support level in October 1922, was at 53. Mack Trucks rallied to 85 in March 1930, which shows only a rally in a bear market.

Packard Motor Car - This stock was a late mover. 1921, low 5; December 1922, high 21; November 1923, low 10; May 1924, low 10. It showed big accumulation between 10 and 16. (See monthly chart, 1923-1927.) In April 1925, crossed 21, the high of 1922, which was the place to buy the stock for a big advance. October and November 1925, high 48; declined to 32 in March 1926. In July 1926, advanced to 45; October 1926, declined to 32, same low as March. There was big accumulation between 33 and 38 from October 1926, to July 1927. In August the big advance started and in October it crossed 48, the high of 1925 and a further big advance followed. From May 1927, when it sold at 34 the last time, every monthly bottom was higher until December 1928, when the top was reached at 163. This was an advance of 130 points without any sign of a change in the main trend and was a great move to pyramid. In March 1929, it declined to 117; May 1929, rallied to 154. In July declined to 128 where it again showed accumulation and good support; in September advanced to 161. The stock was split up on a basis of 5 for one. The new stock sold at 32 in September 1929, equal to 160 for the old stock. In November 1929, the new stock declined to 13, equal to 65 for the old stock, down nearly 100 points from the top. A study of the monthly high and low chart on Packard at the bottom will show you where there was big accumulation, and how the stock had gotten into a strong position to make a big move up after some of the other motor stocks had been leaders in the early part of the Bull Campaign.

Studebaker - This was one of the best and one of the first leaders in the 1921 Bull Campaign. This stock was referred to in TRUTH OF THE STOCK TAPE as being one of the stocks in strongest position. In December 1920, it reached a low of 38; advanced to 141 in 1922. There was a stock dividend declared in 1924. After that the stock acted very much like Packard, as you can see from a monthly chart. After making a high of 68 in November 1925, it declined to 47 in May 1926. Around this level big accumulation took place. It continued in a trading range the greater part of 1926 and 1927. In January 1928, it crossed 68, the high of 1925, and in January 1929, made top at 98 and the main trend turned down. It declined to 38 in November 1929, the same low level where it made bottom in September, October and November 1924, and also the same low level reached in December 1920. This stock had a small rally to 47 in February 1930.

White Motors - This was one of the early leaders which made top in late 1925 and never went higher. 1921, low, 29; then started a second advance in June 1924, and made final top at 104 in August 1925. Distribution continued until October and November 1925, when the main trend turned down. Rallies were very small until April 1926, when it made a low of 52; in August rallied to 64; then another period of distribution took place and the downward trend was resumed. In November 1927, White Motors sold at 30, just one point above the 1921 low and a sign of weakness, but a place to buy for a rally. In April 1929, rallied to 53; declined in November 1929, reaching a low of 28, getting support around the 1927 and 1921 low levels, another place to buy. There was a rally to 43 in April 1930.

Suppose a trader or an investor had bought this stock any time during 1926, 1927 or 1928 just because General Motors was strong and advancing, expecting it to follow General Motors, he would have suffered heavy losses because the trend on White Motors was down, while General Motors showed strong up trend. Learn to never buck the trend. Do not buy one stock in a group to follow another stock unless it shows a strong position. Judge each stock on its own position according to the chart.

OIL STOCKS

Many of the oil stocks made high in 1922 and the early part of 1923, but failed to participate to any great extent in the 1924 to 1929 Bull Campaign. The cause of this was due to overproduction, but the day is coming when this will stop. With the demand constantly increasing, the oils will come into their own as soon as production decreases. Of course, there is a possibility of some new chemical discovery which will take the place of gasoline and hurt the earnings of the oil companies. Nevertheless, the good oil companies should be watched for future possibilities, and when they get active and the trend shows up according to the charts, you should buy them.

Mexican Petroleum - The great bull leader in the 1922 to 1923 Bull Campaign, started up from 85 in August, 1921, and advanced to 322 in December 1922. The stock was exchanged for stock in Pan-American Petroleum Co. Mexican Pete was one of the best oil stocks to buy in 1921 for a big advance as it showed big accumulation and rallied quickly, making higher bottoms and higher tops after low was reached. The fact that there was a very small floating supply made it easy for pools to advance the stock, especially as it possessed real value and merit.

Atlantic Refining -Was another early leader in the 1921 to 1929 Bull Campaign. In January 1923, it reached high at 160 and in July 1924, declined to 79; in February 1925, advanced to 117; and declined in March 1925, to 98. Then followed another rally to June and July 1925, when it reached a high of 116, failing to cross the top of February 1925, which was an indication for a short sale. There was good selling around this level and in August 1925, the stock declined to 97. It advanced to 110 in November 1925, and again declined to 97 in March 1926, which was another place to buy protected with a stop at 94. A quick rally followed and in May 1926, the stock sold at 128. This was a sharp, quick rally and was followed by a quick reversal and a sharp decline to 97 in October 1926. This was the fourth time the stock had made bottom at this level and was good to buy again with stop at 94. In August 1927, it advanced to 131, just 3 points above the top of 1926. This was another sharp top. The trend quickly reversed and the price declined to 96 in February 1928, which was the fifth time it had been supported around this level. It was again a good buy with a stop at 94. Another fast advance followed and in April the stock crossed 1926 and 1927 tops and went up to 140, the top of January 1924, where it met selling for 3 months and in June 1928, declined to 111; then rallied to 141, a new high and closed the month at 139. In July 1928, it advanced to a new high of 143, when you should have bought more stock, as this was an indication for a big advance to follow, because after making so many bottoms at 96 and 97 and then making a new high indicated that it would go very much higher. In October 1928, when it was selling around 238, a stock dividend was declared. In December 1928, the new stock sold as low as 50; then slowly worked up until July 1929, when it made top at 77; declined to 30 in October 1929; rallied to 51 in April 1930.

General Asphalt - This was one of the big leaders in the 1919 Bull Campaign. In July 1922, it made high at 73 and in August 1923, sold down to 23, which was under the 1920 and 1921 lows, an indication that the stock was in a weak position and would not be a leader. In August 1926, high 94; March 1927, high 96; April and May 1928, high 95; August 1929, high 95. Making the same top for 4 consecutive years and failing to go higher was a sure sign for a short sale. The stock declined to 43 in November 1929; rallied to 71 in April 1930.

Houston Oil - This stock has a very small floating supply, and is easily influenced by manipulation. August 1921, low 42; October 1922, high 91; August 1923, low 41. This was the place to buy protected with a stop at 39, because it was the same bottom as 1921. In February 1925, it advanced to 85 and in March and October 1926, made a low of 51.After a long period of accumulation a big move started and in February 1927, it crossed the highs of 1922 and 1925 and a runaway advance followed. In July and October 1927, high 174 and 175. There was distribution near the top and the main trend turned down and this stock was not a leader any more for the balance of this Bull Campaign. In October 1929, the stock declined to 26. A big advance followed from this low level and in March 1930, it advanced to 110. This stock rallied more than any other oil stock of its kind due to the fact that the floating supply of the stock is small.

Pan-American Petroleum "B" - Made low in August 1921, when it sold at 35. In October 1922, advanced to 94, being one of the early leaders, but was never a good leader any time after that. February 1924, low 42; March 1925, advanced to 84; February 1928, declined to 38; then followed a rally to 68 in August 1929, and in the panic declined to 50 in October 1929. You can see that after this stock made top in 1922, while it had rallies, the bull move ended in 1922; therefore, it was not the kind of an oil stock to play for a leader on the bull side.

Phillips Petroleum - Made final high in April 1923, when it sold at 69; never went higher during the bull campaign; worked lower and in November 1929, declined to 24, rallied to 41 in April 1930.

Standard Oil of California - Made high in October 1922, at 135; declared a stock dividend. In August 1923, the new stock sold at 48; then remained in a narrow, trading range, finally advancing to 82 in June 1929; declined to 52 in October 1929, making bottom 4 points above the low of 1923, which showed strong support; rallied to 73 in April 1930. This is one of the best Standard Oil stocks and is good to buy as long as the charts show up trend.

A few of the oils had a rally in July and August 1929, but it was too near the end of the bull campaign and a sharp decline followed. It is plain to see that, with a few exceptions, the man who stuck to oil stocks from 1922 to 1929 had very limited chances for making big profits, and if he continued to trade in oil stocks, he missed many opportunities in other active stocks that were leading in the Bull

Campaign. It pays to stick to the active leaders and you should not wait too long before changing from an inactive stock to an active one.

PUBLIC UTILITIES

This group of stocks led the final grand rush in the 1929 Bull Campaign and put the night cap on the bull market. They were late movers. The last fast move was caused by buying for investment trusts who made some big mistakes and bought stocks near the top. Shorts covered in the last stage of the bull market and the public came in and bought, forcing the public utilities to abnormally high prices and it was only natural that a sharp, severe decline had to follow.

American & Foreign Power - In September 1925, high was 51; in October and November 1926, made a low at 15 : was accumulated in 1927 and part of 1928. In November 1928, crossed 51, the high of 1925, an indication for much higher prices. In September 1929, reached top at 199. The move collapsed and in October 1929, made a low of 50, getting back to the low of 1925, which was a buying point with a stop at 48. In December 1929, American Foreign Power rallied to 101; reacted to 89. In February 1930, advanced again to 101, and failing to cross this top, showed that it should be sold short. In March 1930, it declined to 83.

American Power & Light - November 1924, low 38; January 1926, high 79; March 1926, low 49. It was in an accumulating stage after that until April 1928; crossed 80, the top of 1926, and advanced to 95 in May 1928. Had another period of rest and accumulation until December 1928, when it started up from 76. Made final high at 175 in September 1929. This was a sharp top and like American Foreign Power and U. S. Industrial Alcohol, which were late movers, had a sharp decline. When American Power & Light broke 154 in October, which was under the low for the month of September, it indicated down trend, and if you were short! you should have sold more. In November 1929, it declined to 65. This was the same low level made in February 1928, before the big up move started, and a place to buy. In March 1930, the stock rallied to 119.

Brooklyn Union Gas - Low in 1924, 57; November,1925, high 100; March 1926, low 68; advanced to the highest price in history in August 1929, reaching 248. It made a sharp top, collapsed and a sharp decline followed, reaching low in November 1929, when the stock sold at 99. Then rallied in March 1930, to 178. This was another late mover, but being one of the best public utilities, was good to buy in the panic of 1929.

Standard Gas H Electric- Low 19 in 1923; February 1926, high 69; March 1926, low 51; was in a trading range and showed accumulation until late in 1928, when it started a fast move up. Made final top at 243 in September 1929. A wide-open break followed and in November 1929, it sold as low as 74. A rally followed to April 1930, when it advanced to 128.

These fast moves in the late moving stocks in the last stage of a bull market prove that you must act quickly and get out of longs in the last stage of a bull market, for if you hold on and hope, you will be ruined with heavy losses. The daily and weekly high and low charts will help you to see the change in trend in these rapid movers and enable you to get out of the longs and go short before it is too late.

RUBBER AND TIRE STOCKS

The stocks in this group were not good leaders in the first section of the 1921 to 1929 Bull Campaign. They did not have any very big advances from 1921 to 1923 and some of them made lower levels in 1923 and 1924 than they did in 1921.

Goodrich - Made the same low in 1920 and 1921, selling at 27. In May 1922, rallied to 44. This was a small rally after such a big decline from the 1919 high. In November 1922, declined to 29, which was a sign of weakness getting down so near the 1921 low after having such a small rally. In March 1923, high 41, a lower top than 1922. The trend turned down again and in October 1923, the stock sold at 18. Getting lower than the 1921 low indicated a weak position. In January 1924, rallied to 26, failing to get above the lows of 1920 and 1921; in June 1924, made low at 17 and in September 1924, crossed 26, the last top or Resistance Level and turned the main trend up. This was the place to buy. You could have bought on the double bottom, as the stock made practically the same lows in 1923 and 1924, but the place to buy for a quick advance was after the main trend turned up. In November 1925, it advanced and made high at 74. The main trend turned down again and in November 1926, it declined to 39. Here accumulation took place and the main trend turned up. In January 1928, it reached the high of 99; June 1928, declined to 69, which was the same bottom as it made in September, October and November 1927. There was good support and the advance was resumed. In December 1928, final high was reached at 107. This was a sharp top and the trend turned down quickly and continued down until December 1929, when a low of 39 was made. This was the same low as November 1926, and a Resistance Level, where you should have bought with a stop at 36. Goodrich rallied to 58 in March 1930.

Goodyear - This stock made a low of 5 in 1921, but was slow until 1927 when the upward swing started. January 1928, high 72 ; June 1928, low 45. A fast advance started and reached top in March 1929, making high at 154. This was a sharp top and a sharp, quick decline followed. In October 1929, it declined to 60. A rally followed to March 1930, when the stock reached 96.

U. S. Rubber - 1921 low 41, down 102 points from the 1919 top; April 1922, rallied to 67, a small rally after a big decline and indicated weakness; December 1922, low 46. Making a higher bottom than 1921, this was the place to buy for a rally. March 1923, high 64, a lower top than 1922, and a sign of lower prices. Remember the rule that a stock must cross the highs of the first year of a bull campaign before it indicates any further big advance. In April 1924, declined to a new low at 23. Around this level it was dull and narrow and accumulation took place. In January and February 1925, it advanced to 44, a Resistance Level, where bottoms were made in July, August and September 1923. The stock reacted to 34 and in April 1925, crossed 44 which showed it was in a strong position and the point to buy more. In November 1925, reached high at 97, making a sharp top, and a quick, sharp reaction followed, the main trend turning down. In May 1926, low 51; August 1926, high 68; October 1926, low 52, another buying level against the low of 51 with a stop at 48. In March 1927, made top of rally at 67, a sign of weakness because it failed to cross the high of August 1926. The trend turned down again and in June 1927, reached a low of 37. A rally followed to January 1928, when it made high at 63, another lower top and a sign of lower prices. In June 1928, declined to 27, holding 4 points above the low of 1924, indicating good support. This was a buying level. The trend turned up and in March 1929, made high at 65, 2 points above the 1928 high. Failing to make 3 points higher indicated lower prices, and failing to cross 1926 and 1927 highs around 67 and 68 was a sign of weakness and the stock should have been sold short. A quick decline followed and the main trend turned down again. May 1929, low 46; rallied to 58 in September 1929, and in October 1929, declined to 15, the lowest level since 1907 when it sold at 14. This was a buying level protected with a stop at 12. A rally followed and in April 1930, the stock advanced to 35. This stock had been going down for 5 years or from November 1925, while other stocks were going up. Therefore, liquidation has run its course and U. S. Rubber can go up while other stocks which were late movers decline.

The fact that the Du Ponts control it is a strong argument that it will have a big advance in later years. It will probably go much higher in 1932. This stock is one of the good stocks in the rubber group to buy.

STEEL AND IRON STOCKS

Bethlehem Steel - I have stated before that after a stock has a tremendous advance, it may be many years before it will be a leader in another bull campaign and have big advances. Bethlehem Steel sold at 8 in 1907 and during the war boom sold at 700 in 1916, when a stock dividend was declared and the stock split up. In 1921, the low on the new stock was 40. It advanced to 79 in 1922. Then the trend turned down, and in 1924 it sold at 38 and rallied to 53. In June 1925, sold at 37, a buying level against 38 bottom in 1924. Bethlehem rallied to 50 in November and December 1925; again declined to 37½ in April 1926, which was a support level, and should have been bought with a stop at 35. In August 1926, advanced to 51, but failed to cross the high of 53, which was made in January 1925, another indication that the stock was not ready for any big move up. During September and October 1926, and again in January 1927, Bethlehem sold at 43½, showing a higher support and indicating that the stock was in a stronger position and getting ready to go higher. In April 1927, it crossed 53, the old top, and turned the main trend up, but reacted to 46 in June; then advanced to 66 in September, and reacted to 49 in October 1927; advanced to 69 in April 1928, another indication that it was going higher; had its last reaction to 52 in June 1928. From this level the big advance started and it made a high of 140 in August 1929.

Like all late movers, it made a sharp top and a fast decline followed to November 1929, when it sold at 79. Then rallied to 110 in April 1930. Thus you can see that Bethlehem Steel, which had been a leader in the previous bull campaign was a late mover in the 1929 Bull Campaign. While U. S. Steel and U. S. Cast Iron Pipe had led in the early part of the 1921 to 1929 Bull Campaign and continued to work higher, Bethlehem Steel had remained in a narrow, trading range, as you can see from a chart, which shows plainly that from 1921 to 1927, it never indicated that it was ready for any big advance.

Learn to watch your charts and wait for a definite indication before getting into a stock. Only make your trades when a stock is active and crosses old Resistance Levels. In this way you will avoid being tied up with inactive stocks and will make profits much quicker.

Colorado Fuel & Iron - This is another stock which you would have picked - if you had watched it at the bottom and applied the rules - as being one of the best to buy for a rally after the panicky decline in 1929, for the following reasons: Colorado Fuel had made top in July 1927, therefore when it reached bottom in November 1929, it had been declining over 2 years, and naturally, would be better liquidated and in position to rally quicker than U. S. Steel, which had only made top in September

1929, and had only declined 2½ months. It made low on November 13, 1929, selling at 28. This was the same low as it made on March 26, 1926. However, Vanadium at this time failed to go as low as the March 1926, levels by 8½ points, therefore, it showed a better support even than Colorado Fuel. Colorado Fuel & Iron rallied to 39 on December 9, 1929, and on December 20 and 23, declined to 32, making a higher bottom, showing it was being well supported and was good to buy. During the weeks ending November 23 to December 28, it made lows around 31½ to 32, showing that there was good support during all these weeks. In the early part of January 1930, Colorado Fuel crossed 40, the high of December 9, 1929, and then worked higher, making higher tops and higher bottoms until April 1930, when it advanced to 76, up 48 points from the low of November. During the time that Vanadium Steel advanced 87 points from the bottom and Colorado Fuel 48 points, U.S. Steel only advanced 42 points. One of the reasons for this was that U. S. Steel, with a volume of over 8 million shares, required heavier buying power and a strong pool to put it up, and naturally, would meet much heavier selling on the way up than a stock that only had a few hundred thousand shares outstanding.

Crucible Steel - This was one of the "war babies" and sold at 110⅞ in 1915; then declined to 46 in 1917; made a low of 52 in 1918 and 1919; had a big advance during the 1919 Bull Campaign and made final high in April 1920, when it sold at 278¾. A study of the yearly high and low chart on page 99 will show you how this stock had been accumulated for years and was in position for a big advance when it crossed the old levels. When the stock reached the high in April 1920, a stock dividend was declared. The new stock sold at 49 in August 1921. It was one of the last stocks to make bottom around August 25 1921. In September 1922, advanced to 98; then turned the trend down and in May 1924, made a low of 48, a buying level, being one point under 1921 low, but the fact that it got back this low showed that it was not going to be one of the early leaders in the 1921 to 1929 Bull Campaigns, because it had been a big leader in the 1919 Bull Campaign. It then worked up very slowly, and in March 1927, reached 96; then declined to 80, and in August, September and October 1927, advanced to 96 again, failing to cross the top of 1922, the first year of the Bull Campaign. In July 1928, declined to 70; became dull and narrow, and was accumulated. The main trend turned up again and final high was reached in August 1929, when it sold at 121. This was a late mover at the tail end of a bull market, and naturally made a sharp top and a collapse followed, declining in November 1929, to 71, getting within one point of the low of July 1928, which was a buying level, protected with a stop.

You might ask why Crucible Steel was not a leader in the 1921 to 1929 Bull Campaign. The reason for this was that it was a leader in 1915 and 1916 and again a leader in 1919 and 1920, and had an extreme advance to 278 when the stock was split up, therefore, it was not one of the stocks that could be expected to have another big advance in the next bull campaign. "Every dog has his day." This stock was a good dog and had its day; besides it had been split up and distributed. Watch for the new stocks with opportunities and those that have not been leaders, and avoid getting hung up, expecting some stock that has led before to be a leader later when the indications on the chart show it is not going to lead. Make up a monthly chart from high and low prices given in charts and study it.

Republic Iron & Steel - This stock was a late mover in the 1919 Bull Campaign, making top in November 1919, at 145. In June 1921, it declined to 42; May 1922, advanced to 78; November 1922, again declined to 44, a support level, being 2 points above the low of 1921 and a place to buy with a stop. In March 1923, advanced to 66. Failing to get as high as 1922 showed weakness and indicated that it was not going to lead at this time. In June 1923, declined to 41, one point under the low of June 1921. While this was a support level and a place to buy again, at the same time it indicated that the stock was not yet ready to have any big advance. In February 1924, advanced to 61, again making a lower top than the previous high. In June 1924, again declined to 42, a buying level; in August advanced to 50, and in October declined to 42, back to the support level. A stock is always good to buy at these levels until it breaks 3 points under its previous level. Three points under the first low level at 42 would make the stop at 39. In January 1925, it advanced to 64, and in April, May and June 1925, again declined to 43, getting support around the same low level, and still a place to buy with stop at 39. In January 1926, made high at 63, failing to cross the top of 1925. In May 1926, it again declined to 44, getting support at a slightly higher level, a good indication for a better advance to follow so long as the stock held these Resistance Levels. In August 1926, high 63, still failing to cross the 1925 and January 1926, high levels. Thus you can see that during 1921 to 1926, bottoms were made at 44 to 41 and from 1923 to 1926, tops at 63 to 66. This showed that the stock was supported every time it declined below 44, but that someone sold enough to check the advance when it advanced up to around 63.

In February 1927, it crossed 66 and in March made a high of 75¾, but again failed to reach 78, the high of 1922, the first year of the bull campaign. Now, if 78 could be exceeded, it would indicate much higher prices. From March 1927, the trend turned down and bottom was not reached until June 1928, when it again sold at 50. From this level a fast upward move developed. In September 1928, crossed 78, and here would have been a place to buy more stock. The trend continued up to September 1929, when it reached a high of 146¾, just 2 points above the 1919 top. Here you should have sold out longs and gone short at the 1919 top, with a stop 3 points away, and your stop would not have been caught. A fast decline followed to November 1929, when the stock sold at 63, getting support at the same level at which it formerly had been sold on the way up when it had been rallying to these points. In April 1930, the stock rallied to 82.

U. S. Pipe & Foundry - Formerly U. S. Cast Iron Pipe, was one of the early and good leaders in the 1921 to 1929 Bull Campaign for the following reasons: (1) It had been accumulated for years (see yearly chart, 1902-1930); (2) there was a very small capitalization of only 120,000 shares and much of this stock was not outstanding, or was closely held; (3) the earnings were good and the pools found it easy to advance the stock. This is the kind of stock that is dangerous to sell short when it shows up trend. In August 1921, low was 12. (See monthly, weekly and daily charts) The trend turned up in January 1922, and reached high at 39 in August 1922. This was the same high as it made in 1919 and above all tops except 1906, which was at 53. In July 1923, it made last low at 20, 3 points above the 1922 low, which showed good support and was a place to buy. The trend turned up again and in October 1923, crossed 40, above the 1919 and 1922 highs. This was the point to buy more stock and to pyramid on the way up as the stock showed it was in a strong position and very active, making higher bottoms and higher tops.

In November 1923, it crossed 53 and went to 58 the same month, getting 5 points above the 1906 high, the record. This was the time and place to buy more of the stock. It never declined to 53 again until it sold at 250 in February 1925. Then followed a sharp, severe decline to April 1925, when the price reached 132. The trend turned up again and it sold at 227 in November 1925. In May 1926, it declined to 150, getting support 18 points higher than the low of April 1925. The weekly and daily charts showed support here and bottom. The up trend was resumed and in August 1926, top was made at 248, just 2 points lower than the top of February 1925. This was the place to sell out longs and go short with a stop at 253. A sharp decline followed, and in October 1926, it sold at 191. The weekly and daily charts showed bottom here.

In December 1926, it advanced to 239; January 1927, declined to 202; rallied to 225 in February, made bottom at 207 in March 1927. Making a higher bottom showed that it was getting in position to go higher. An advance followed, which culminated in May 1927, when top was made at 246, just 2 points lower than the August 1926 top. There was a big distribution around this level and this was the place to go short again. In July 1927, the stock declined to 191, the same low as October 1926, a buying level with a stop at 188. A rally followed and top was made in December 1927, at 225. In February 1928, the stock declined to 191, the third time at this same low level and a place to cover shorts and buy with a stop at 188. A rapid advance followed, and in May 1928, the stock crossed 250, the high of February 1925, and making 253 indicated much higher prices and you should have bought more even at this high level. In April 1928, it made final top at 300 and a sharp decline followed, reaching 230 in June 1928. A stock dividend was declared and the new stock sold at 38 in December 1928 ; rallied to 48; declined to 38 in February 1929, making a double bottom. Final high was reached in March 1929, when the new stock sold at 55. Heavy selling appeared around this top and a fast decline followed. The main trend continued down until November 1929, when it made a low at 12, the same low as August 1921, and a buying level. The stock rallied to 38 in April 1930. (See yearly charts, 1902-1930)

U. S. Steel - This has always been a good stock to trade in because it nearly always remains longer at tops or bottoms and gives traders a chance to buy or sell with a close stop loss order.

In the 1921 to 1929 Bull Campaign, Steel was an early leader and also a late leader. It had three important moves, or three important bull campaigns, during the 8 years from 1921 to 1929. June 1921, low 71; high for the year 1921 was 86. During July and August 1921, the stock remained in a 4-point range, showing big accumulation. Each month after June, the bottoms were progressive or higher and the tops higher. In January 1922, it crossed 86, the high of 1921, which indicated higher prices. In October 1922, Steel made first top at 111; reacted to 100; in March 1923, rallied to 109. Failing to reach the top of October 1922, was an indication for a short sale. The main trend turned down and in July 1923, it declined to 86 and held for 4 months, making bottoms at this same level, showing good support and big accumulation. This was the time to buy with a stop at 83. The trend turned up in November 1923, and made top at 109 in February 1924, the same top as March 1923. This was the place for selling short with a stop at 112. It declined in May and June 1924, and made low at 95, both months. The weekly and daily charts showed accumulation and bottom.

In July 1924, the trend turned up, and in August it reached 111, the high of March 1923.
A small reaction followed to 105 in October 1924, and the price crossed 112 in November. This was the place to buy more for a further advance. In January 1925, high was 129. Good selling took place around this level and in March U. S. Steel declined to 113, and made the same low in April; made one point higher in May and June, showing good support. The upward trend was resumed in July and the price reached 139 in November 1925, the highest in history, being 3 points above the 1917 high.

This was an indication for higher prices later, but profit-taking checked the advance around this level for 3 months and finally the stock declined to 115 in April 1926. Here big accumulation took place and in June the main trend turned up, and again a fast advance followed. Crossing 140 was the place to buy more. In August 1926, it made high at 159. This was a sharp top, made on big volume, and a quick decline followed. In October 1926, made low at 134. Here good buying was encountered and the trend started up again. In November 1926, a stock dividend of 40 per cent was declared and the old stock advanced to 176 in May 1927.

The new stock started at 117 in December 1926, and sold at 111¼ in January 1927. This was a support level, as the lows in March and April 1925, were 113. There was 3 months' accumulation around this level, and in March 1927, it reached high at 161. Failing to get 3 points above the old high level was an indication to sell it short. A fast decline followed and in October it reached 129. This was only one month's reaction. The bottom was higher the next month. In December 1927, top was made at 159. This was the place to go short again. The stock reacted to 138; rallied to 154 in April 1928, and failed to cross the top of December 1927, and should have been sold short again. A decline followed to 133 in June 1928. This bottom was 3 points higher than the low of October 1927, and a sign of strength. A quick rally followed; the trend turned up in August and crossed the tops of 154 and 155 and continued to 172 in November 1928; declined to 150 in December 1928. This was a quick, sharp decline and a fast advance followed. In January 1929, it made top at 192; reacted in February to 169; then advanced to 193 in March, getting only one point above the January and February highs, a sign of heavy selling and a signal to sell short with a stop 3 points away. A decline followed and in May 1929, bottom was made at 162½. In the last week of the decline the market was dull and narrow and the volume of sales for the week was only 220,000 shares. In the week ending June 8, 1929, the low was 165 and the high 171. In the following week the low was the same, 165, a sign of good support at this level, this being the second week of higher bottoms. The high for the week was 177, showing up trend again, and the volume of sales increased, showing heavy buying.

In the week ending July 13, Steel crossed 193, making a new high. This was the place to buy more because the volume of sales was increasing and the market was very active. Every week following, Steel made higher bottoms and higher tops. In the weeks ending August 10 and 17, the sales exceeded a million shares. August 24, first top was at 260½. The sales that week were 800,000 shares. There was a quick reaction to 251½ and the volume of sales was only 391,000 for the week. A quick rally followed, making final top on September 3, 1929, at 261¾. This time the stock failed to get 3 points above the top made on August 24, a sign for lower prices. A fast decline followed to 246 the same week; the sales were 561,000 about 170,000 shares more than the sales during the week that the stock reacted from 260½ to 251½. This was a sign of good selling. When the price broke 251, more should have been sold because this was the first time that a weekly bottom had been broken since Steel started up from 162½. On September 3, 1929, the day Steel reached top, the sales were 129,000. This showed very poor buying at such a high level and indicated short covering and public buying while the insiders were selling. On October 3, 1929, Steel declined to 206½. A quick rally followed and on October 11, 1929, it advanced to 234. This was only one week's rally and the following week it declined under heavy selling to 208. There was only a small rally on short covering from this level. On October 29, 1929, Steel declined to 162½ on sales of 307,000 shares for the day. A sharp rally followed to October 31, when Steel advanced to 193½ on sales of 100,000 shares, the range for the day being 5½ points. A decline followed and on November 13, U. S. Steel declined to 150. The sales that day were 97,000, small volume, showing that liquidation had run its course.

A quick rally followed to October 21, when Steel reached 171½ . It declined on December 2, to 159¼; advanced and crossed 172, the high of October 21; and on December 9 reached top at 189 on sales of 355,000, the largest of any day since October 24, showing that there was good selling and that a reaction should follow, especially after it had rallied 39 points from the bottom. The fact that the stock failed to cross the top of October 31 at 193½ indicated lower prices to follow. A fast decline took place and on December 23 Steel sold at 156¾ on sales of 111,000 for the day. The small volume of sales again indicated that liquidation had run its course and that the market was making bottom.

This being a higher bottom than November 13 indicated good support. An advance started, the daily trend turned up, and early in January 1930, the weekly trend turned up. February 14, high 189, sales 154,000, same top as December 9. A reaction followed to February 17, when the stock sold at 184½; then rallied on February 18 to 189½, sales 120,000 shares. Failing to get one point above the old top was a sign of weakness and a decline followed.

On February 25, it sold at 177; rallied to 184 on March 1; then declined to 178¾ on March 5 and 6; rallied on March 7, making top at 184 again; March 14 declined to 177¾, still holding above the low level of 177 made on February 25. A rally followed on March 19, when Steel sold at 188¼ with a total sales of 179,000. On March 20 the high was 188½, with sales of 67,000. March 21 high 191, sales 186,000. This was the largest number of sales for some time and having crossed 189, the high of December 9, 1929, and 189½ the high of February 18, 1930, Steel indicated that it would go higher after a reaction. On March 24, U. S. Steel sold at 192¼ on sales of 126,900, and on March 25, advanced to a high of 193¼ on sales of 83,600. Then reacted to 189½ on March 27. Failing to break back under the old top levels at 189 made on December 9, 1929, and 189½ on February 18, 1930, indicated that it was getting support and was going higher. On April 7 advanced to 198½, sales 106,000 shares; April 8 declined to 193¼ on sales of 114,000 shares; April 10 advanced to 197⅞ on sales of 103,000 shares. Failing to cross the high level of April 7 and being so near the even figure of 200 where there is always good selling, indicated a reaction to follow. When the stock can advance to 200, it will then indicate higher prices. The low level of April 3 was 192⅝ and of April 8, 193¼; should the stock break under these levels before crossing 200, it will indicate lower prices.

Vanadium Steel - This stock was a creeper during the early part of the 1921 to 1929 Bull Campaign. When a stock creeps or moves very slowly for a long time, but at the same time makes higher bottoms and higher tops, it will eventually have a wild, runaway market or rapid advance. Creeping stocks invariably wind up with a final grand rush on short covering and public buying. These fast moves are really an advertising campaign which get the public in near the top. Remember that stocks are put up to sell, and don't forget that when they are sold, they go down, so use stop loss orders and reverse position when the trend reverses. Vanadium was one of the new stocks that came into prominence late in 1919 and made a high of 97 in April 1920. Then declined to 20 in June 1924. Then the up move started, making higher bottoms and higher tops; crossed 60 in January 1928, and made a high of 116 in February 1929. In November 1929, declined to a low of 37½. If you were watching the steel stocks and looking over the steel group to pick the best stocks to buy, Vanadium was the stock you would have selected, if you had followed the rules laid down in TRUTH OF THE STOCK TAPE.

At the low price of 37½ in November 1929, it was back to the same level where bottoms were made in November 1926, and January 1927, when the last low level was reached at 37, from which the stock started a big advance. It became more active and worked upward until February 1929, when it reached high at 116. Another reason for buying it was that the 1929 bottom was 8½ points higher than the bottom reached in the panicky decline of March 26, 1926, and another reason for expecting it to be bottom and buying it was that the top reached in February 1929, was made much earlier than U. S. Steel and some other stocks which did not make top until August and September 1929. Therefore, Vanadium had been going down 8 months before the other stocks and naturally would be in position to rally sooner and lead in the next advance. Another good and sufficient reason for selecting it as being one of the stocks to buy for an advance was that there is only about 300,000 shares of the stock outstanding. This small floating supply makes it easier for their stock to advance, especially when you compare it with U. S. Steel, which has over 8 million shares outstanding. Another reason is that the company has practically a monopoly on Vanadium.

The low on Vanadium Steel in May 1929, was 68. It had declined from 116 to this level. Then from 68 it rallied to 100 in September 1929, from which it declined to the low of 37½ in November. A natural rally point would be to around 68, the low point of May 1929, but we have to look up the last point from which the stock declined. Vanadium sold at 48½ on October 29, the day of the big panicky decline. Then on October 31, it rallied to 62. From this level it declined to 37½ on November 13; then rallied to December 9, reaching 61½, failing to cross the high level of October 31. When it could cross this level, it would indicate considerably higher prices. From the top of December 9, another decline followed, and on December 20, Vanadium declined to 44½, making a higher bottom and indicating that it was one of the good stocks to buy, because on the secondary decline it did not get as low as the last bottom. After the low in December, Vanadium started making higher bottoms and higher tops on the daily high and low chart. On January 25, 1930, advanced to 51½ and closed at the top on sales of 16,000; January 27, crossed 62, the high of October 31 and December 9, 1929, advanced to 64¼ on January 27 and closed at the top on sales of 25,000, indicating big buying at advancing prices; January 30 reached high at 69½. February 4, declined to 62½, down 7 points from the top, which was the first reaction of this much since the stock started up from the low of 44½. The advance was resumed and on February 14 reached a high of 73½ on sales of 34,000 shares, the largest volume of the month, an indication of top for a reaction.

February 25, declined to 65½. At the bottom the sales were only 7,700 which indicated that there was not much heavy selling and showed support and place to buy. It was down 8 points from the top and just one point more than the reaction which occurred from January 30 to February 4, 1930. The stock started up again, making higher bottoms and higher tops each day, and on March 6th crossed 74 on sales of 26,000 shares. Getting over the top of February 14 was a sign for much higher prices. Now, the next point to watch was the last high at 86½ which was made on the rally of October 11, 1929, from which the big decline followed. On March 10, Vanadium advanced to 88½ on sales of 28,000, closing at 86½, indicating higher prices, having gone through the high of October 11, 1929. After making 88½, it reacted to 82 early on March 12, 1930, then started up the same day and advanced to 92½ on sales of 28,000. The next point to watch was the high made in March and April 1929, when the stock rallied to 100; then had a sharp reaction and advanced again on September 13, 1929, to 100, on a large volume of sales, 59,000, and a rapid decline followed. On March 21, 1930, the stock crossed 100, on sales of 46,800. Crossing 100, the next important top was the extreme high of 116, which was made on February 9, 1929. On March 25, 1930, Vanadium ,crossed 116, the high of 1929, and advanced to 124½, the sales being 54,500 at the highest price it had ever sold.

The stock opened that day at 118, advanced to 124½, declined to 114 and closed at the low, being down 10½ points from the high at the top. This was a sign of weakness and indicated lower prices, and also the volume being so large indicated that heavy selling had been encountered. Nevertheless, the fact must not be overlooked that the main trend on the weekly, monthly and daily charts was still up, but the fact that the previous reaction had not exceeded 7½ points and this reaction being 10½ points in one day showed that the stock was being heavily sold.

It is important to watch the volume at the extreme high and low levels in order to have a comparison in determining when the volume indicates that the stock is making top or bottom. The largest volume of sales for 1929 was on February 7, when sales reached 68,800 shares. On February 8, when the stock reached top for the year at 116, sales were 43,800. The two days, totaling over 108,000 shares, indicated that there was heavy selling and that the stock was making top. During the week ending February 9, the total sales on Vanadium were 175,800. This was a very large percentage of sales, considering that the total capital stock outstanding is only a little over 300,000 shares, therefore, over two-thirds of the capital stock had changed hands. This certainly indicated good selling. The next important point to study on volume is the week ending September 14, 1929, when Vanadium advanced to 100. The sales this week were 138,400, which indicated good selling and top, especially as the main trend had already turned down. During the week ending October 26, sales were 56,400, and during the week ending November 2, sales were 50,600. During the week ending November 9, sales were 17,200 and during the week ending November 16, sales were 29,000. Notice that the last two weeks when the stock was making final bottom, the volume of sales was very small, which indicated that liquidation had run its course.

During the week ending December 2, sales were 31,000, and during the week ending December 14, sales were 21,000. During the week ending December 21, when the stock declined to 44½, sales were only 19,000 shares, and in view of the fact that the stock made a higher bottom, this showed there was not much pressure to sell and that there was good support. During the next three weeks the stock showed good accumulation, and the volume of sales was only 12,000 to 13,000 shares per week, which indicated that somebody was just taking what stock was offered and was not yet bidding for it, but that there was not much stock pressing for sale. When the advance was resumed, it was on increased volume of sales. During the week ending March 8, 1930, the high was 78 and the sales were 84,000 shares. During the week ending March 15 the high was 96 and the sales 145,000 shares. During the week ending March 22, the high was 107 and sales 165,000 shares. During the week ending March 29, the high was 124½ and sales 206,000 shares. This was the largest volume of sales since February 9, 1929, and exceeding this week in total sales at the highest level in history indicated that there was heavy selling and profit-taking, and it was time to at least watch for a reaction in the stock from November 13, 1929, to March 25, 1930, Vanadium advanced 87 points. Now, it is always important to watch the greatest reaction from any point as a stock moves up or the greatest rally as a stock declines. The first reaction from the first sharp rally was the largest, that is, the top on December 9, 1929, was 61½, and the low of the reaction on December 20, was 44½, which equaled a decline of 17 points. The reactions following this were 7 and 8 points, showing that the stock was supported and not allowed to react as much after it got higher than it was at low levels. This indicated a bull market. Considering that on March 25, 1930, the stock broke back 10½ points in one day, the next important point to watch for a bottom or a rally would be 17 points down from the top of 124½, or around 107½. Breaking more than 17 points from this or any other top, the next important point to watch for a reaction would be about 22 to 25 points down from the top.

It is also important to notice the length of time required to make a reaction. During the time that Vanadium reacted 7 and 8 points, it required from 7 to 10 days to complete the reaction; in other words, more than 7 to 10 days expired from the time the first top was reached until it was exceeded again. After Vanadium reached 124½ on March 25, it reacted the same day 10½ points. This was a sign of weakness, especially when you consider the heavy volume of trading. It continued to work lower until April 5, when it sold at 103½ , down 20 points from the top; then rallied to 117½ on April 11. The next important point to watch is 124½. If it crosses this level, it will indicate much higher, probably 150, but should it break 103½, the last support level, it would then indicate a further reaction. But do not forget that Vanadium has made the highest prices of history in 1930 and that the main trend is up; therefore, you will have to watch for distribution before determining that it has made final top.

STORES AND MERCHANDISING STOCKS

Jewel Tea -This stock was a very late mover in the 1921 to 1929 Bull Campaign, but after it passed out of the accumulating stage it had a big advance, with only small reactions, and was one of the best stocks to buy and pyramid from 1925 to 1929. In November, 1925, the last low was made at 15 and the advance started continuing to November 1928, when the stock reached 179, advancing 164 points without ever reaching 2 months or declining 5 points under any previous month's bottom. During this time the main trend never turned down and there was no reason for selling out. Just figure out how much you could have made pyramiding, buying every 10 points up, and if you kept stop loss order 5 points under the bottom of the previous month, it would never have been caught until the stock advanced 164 points from where the main trend turned up.

Jewel Tea had 6 years of accumulation at low levels before the big move started. Examine yearly charts for the years 1916-1930 and monthly high and low charts for 1920-1930. The stock made a high of 96 in 1916 and did not participate in the 1919 Bull Campaign, the trend continuing down until December, 1920, when it reached a low of $3.00 per share. It is important to note each year's high and low prices. 1920 high 22, low 3; 1921 high 12, low 4; 1922 high 22, low 10; 1923 high 24, low 16; 1924 high 23, low 17; 1925 high 26, low 17. Each year the bottom was higher, showing good support and indicating that eventually the stock was going much higher. Note that the 1920 high and the 1922 high were the same, the high price being 22. My rule is that a stock must advance 3 points above the high of the second year of the bull campaign in order to indicate higher prices, therefore Jewel Tea would have to sell at 25 to indicate that it had crossed the Resistance Level and that higher prices would follow. From 1922 to the end of 1925, the stock was in a range from 16 to 23 most of the time and you could not have made much money trading in it, even if you bought at the bottom and sold at the top. If you had bought near the bottom with the intention of holding it for the long pull, after waiting six years your patience would have been exhausted, because you would miss so many greater opportunities in other stocks, which were early leaders, that you probably would have sold it out in disgust.

During the time that this stock was making a range of 10 points between high and low, many other stocks had advanced from 50 to 300 points. What rule should you use in order to catch this big move at the right time and not have to wait years and wear out your patience? You should use my rule of buying after a stock crosses 3 points over the high of the first year of the bull campaign, or the following year after a stock has made extreme low. The high in 1920 and in 1922 was 22, therefore you would have to wait until the stock could advance 3 points higher, or to 25, before it would indicate that the big upswing should start. During 1922, 1923, and 1924, it advanced to 22 to 24 several times but did not make 25. In July, August, and September 1925, the low was 14¾; in October rallied to 21; in November reacted to 15, the last low level before the big advance started; in December 1925, great activity started with increasing volume of sales, which is always a sign that a big move is on. The stock advanced to 25, crossing all Resistance Levels since 1920. This was the place to buy and the stock never reacted to 22 again.

104

The main trend continued up until November 1928, when it made top at 179, advancing 164 points in 3 years, which was only natural after 6 years of accumulation at low levels. The more time consumed in accumulation, the bigger the advance. The same rule applies to stocks that remain many years at the top, while distribution is taking place, but remember that many stocks make sharp tops and distribution or liquidation takes place on the way down. After Jewel Tea reached top in November 1928, it made a sharp top; had a quick decline; turned the main trend down and a stock dividend was declared. The trend continued down and the new stock sold at 39 in November 1929. Note that the last low level in November 1926, was 39, therefore, the stock received support at the same level and was good to buy with a stop at 36. It rallied to 59 in March 1930.

Montgomery Ward - This was a late leader. It made about the same low around 12 for three years, 1920, 1921 and 1922, and the highs during these years were 25 to 27. Montgomery Ward acted very much like Jewel Tea but started up sooner. During the month of May 1924, the range was only one point for the entire month, the low being 22 and the high 23. This indicated that the stock had come to a dead standstill and that buying and selling were about equal and very little business doing one way or the other. When a stock gets this narrow, great activity nearly always follows. In June 1924, the advance started with increased volume of sales and the price reached 29, which was over the top of the past 3 years. This was a buying level and a big advance followed. In December 1925, it made a high of 84; May 1926, declined to 56; had several months of accumulation, and in August 1927, the trend turned up again. The sure buying level was at 73 and again when it crossed 84, the high of 1925, which it did in November 1927, and advanced to 112 in the same month. During November 1928, the final high was reached at 439⅞. From February 1927, when the last low was made at 60, there was never a time when the stock sold one point lower than a previous month's low level. This showed plainly that the main trend was up all the time and you should have pyramided all the way up.

The stock advanced 380 points before the trend turned down again. From the top in November 1928, a sharp decline followed, turning the main trend down. A stock dividend was declared and the new stock met selling around 156, where it made top in January and February 1929. The main trend continued down until January 15, when it reached a low of 38⅝; then rallied to 48 on January 31; declined to 38¼ on March 24, just ⅜ lower than the low of January 15, 1930.

It is important to study the movements at tops and bottoms and the volume of sales on Montgomery Ward from October 24, 1929, to March 31, 1930. October 24, 1929, was the date of the first Wall Street panic in October. Montgomery Ward declined to 50 on sales of 338,000 shares, which was the largest volume for one day at any time since the stock started down from 138. On October 25, a quick rally followed and it advanced to 77 on sales of 166,000 shares, just about one-half the sales recorded on the decline of the previous day, which showed that the buying on this rally was not as good as the selling on the day of heavy liquidation. Another decline followed and on October 29, the day of the great Wall Street panic, it sold at 49 on sales of 285,000 shares, getting one point under the low of October 24, which showed support and indicated an advance. A quick rally followed to October 31 and the stock advanced to 79 on sales of 138,000 shares. The stock failing to advance 3 points above the high of October 25 and the volume of sales being so small at the top indicated that there was not good buying and longs should have been sold out and the stock sold short. On November 13, 1929, when the majority of stocks made average lows, Montgomery Ward again declined to 49, the same low level as October 29, on sales of 112,000 shares. This was the third time at this low level and the volume of sales was very small, indicating that liquidation was much less or had about run its course for the present.

On December 9, it advanced to 67 on sales of 141,000 shares for the day. Failing by 10 points to reach the high of the previous rally and the volume of sales being so small on the advance indicated that there was not much good buying and still showed main trend down. On December 20, it declined to a new low of 43 on sales of 323,000 shares, the largest of any day since October 24. Making a new low indicated that it was in a weak position and that liquidation had broken out again. On December 31 it rallied to 50 on sales of 48,000 for the day. This was a feeble rally and the volume of sales was small, showing that the buying was not very good. This top at 50 was the same level where bottoms were made on October 24, October 29, and November 13, thus the former support level had become a selling level. On January 15, 1930, Montgomery Ward declined to a new low level of 38⅝ on sales of 307,000 shares. This was heavy liquidation and indicated that stop loss orders had been caught.

It is important here to note that in March 1925, it started up from a low of 41, therefore, when it declined to 38⅝ it failed by ⅝ to get 3 points under the low from which it started and indicated a support level, at least for a rally. On January 31, it advanced to 48 on sales of 133,000 shares, failing to reach the high of December 31, 1929. This was an indication that the stock was still not being bought in sufficient volume to put it higher. The next point to watch would be the last high at 50. If it could cross this level of 50 and make 53, it would indicate higher; but it did not, and on February 14 declined to 43 on sales of 55,000. This was a sign that liquidation had pretty well run its course for the present, and making a higher bottom indicated a rally. On March 3, it advanced to 48 on sales of 190,000 shares. This was the same top as it made on January 31 and failing to cross it indicated weakness. Having made one top at 50 and two tops at 48, then you would figure that if it should make 51, crossing 3 points above the last two tops, it would indicate higher. After March 3 the stock began working lower and on March 24 declined to 38½ on sales of 110,000 shares. Now, compare this with January 15, when the low was 38⅝ and the sales were 307,000 shares. The fact that when it made lower, the sales were only 110,000 shares, showed that the liquidation was not as heavy and that the stock was nearing the point for a rally. On March 28, it declined to 35½ on sales of 111,000. This volume of sales again indicated that liquidation had about run its course.

It is important to look back and see the price from which every big move starts. In August and September, 1924, it made last low at 34 and in October 1924, the low was 35. Therefore, around 35 was a buying level with stop at 32. The stock rallied to 44½ on April 10, and when it can advance to 51, getting 3 points above the previous high levels, it will indicate a further advance. The fact that Montgomery Ward was a late mover in the 1929 Bull Campaign and a stock dividend having been declared, is the reason why it is making bottom later than other stocks and not showing much rallying power.

Sears Roebuck - This was one of the early leaders in the store group in the 1921 to 1929 Bull Campaign. From a low of 55 in 1921, the stock began working up and continued to make higher bottoms and higher tops until the early part of 1926 when it advanced to 241. A stock dividend was declared after the stock reached the high level. Thus you will see that Sears Roebuck was an early leader and had gone up 186 points before Jewel Tea started its big advance. Yet, Jewel Tea advanced176 points from 1921 low to the high in 1928. Sears Roebuck had a second bull campaign after the new stock was accumulated in 1926 and 1927. In January 1926, Sears Roebuck reached a high of 59 and in March, declined to 44. In September 1926, made a high of 58, failing to cross the high of January 1926. In October 1926, it declined to 50; held in a narrow range of accumulation until July 1927. Failing to get back to the low of March 1926, showed good support and indicated higher prices later. In July 1927, it crossed 60, over the highs of 1926, which was the place to buy. A fast move followed and at no time did the stock break 3 points under the previous month's bottom until it made final high at 197 in November 1928. This was a sharp top and a rapid decline followed. The main trend turned down and it sold at 140 in March 1929; rallied to 174 in July 1929; made the same high levels in July, August and September, showing heavy selling and big distribution. The main trend turned down again in September, and in November declined to 80. A quick rally followed to 108 in December 1929; then a second decline to 83, making a higher bottom, showing good support. From this level a rally followed to February 1930, when the stock reached 100; then reacted to 81 in April 1930, but failed to break the low of November 1929, which was a buying level.

Woolworth - This stock was one of the best early leaders as well as one of the best late leaders in the 1921 to 1929 Bull Campaign. It made low in 1920 while many other stocks did not make low until 1921. Making low early in the bear campaign indicated that it would be an early leader in the bull campaign. It made a higher bottom at 105 in 1921, a sure sign of strength. In 1924 it advanced to 345, when a stock dividend was declared. The new stock made a low of 73 in 1924. The trend turned up and it advanced to 220 in October 1925; declined to 189 in January 1926; then advanced to 222. Failing to get 3 points above the old top indicated weakness and the trend turned down again. In May 1926, it sold at 135 ; then started up again. In November 1926, high 196; another stock dividend was declared. In February 1927, the new stock made a low of 118. There was good support and the stock began making higher tops and higher bottoms and the trend continued up until July 1929, when top was reached at 334. Previous to this, in April 1929, another stock dividend was declared. The new stock made bottom at 85 in April and May 1929; then worked higher until September 1929, when final top was reached at 103¾. Heavy selling occurred around this level and big distribution took place. The main trend turned down in early October, and it declined to 52½ in November 1929.

From this you will see that a stock which was considered the best in the store group lost just about one-half its value in less than two months. Therefore, never hold on to good stocks when the main trend is down or when there is a panic on. The best stocks go down in a panic and a man who holds on and hopes when the trend turns down will go broke. After Woolworth sold for 52¼, it rallied to 80 in December 1929; then started down again selling as low as 60 in February 1930. When it broke 95 in October 1929, it was a short sale and again breaking 84, under 3 months' bottoms, it should have been sold short again. Remember my rule that stocks are never too good to sell short and never too high to buy if the trend is up and never too low to sell short as long as the trend is down. The money is made by going with the trend and not by following sentiment.

SUGAR STOCKS

This is one of the groups of stocks that failed to advance much during the 1921 to 1929 Bull Campaign. The price of raw sugar reached 26 cents a pound in 1919 and in the Spring of 1920. After that the price continued to work lower every year, subject to rallies. The fact that raw sugar prices were declining made earnings poor for most of the sugar companies. Besides, they had bought plantations during the war boom, when sugar was at high prices, and had paid high prices for the land, which kept them from making big profits as sugar prices declined. The price of raw sugar worked lower from the 1920 high to 1930, when the price reached 1¾ cents per pound. Sugar stocks were late movers in the 1919 and 1920 Bull Campaign, some of them making final high in the Spring of 1920. Then a fast decline followed.

American Beet Sugar - June 1921, low 26; August 1922, and February 1923, high 49. Heavy selling occurred around this level and the stock declined in August 1923, to 25. This was below the 1921 low level and indicated that there was very little support and that the main trend was down. However, 25 was a support level for a rally. In February 1924, the stock advanced to 49, the same high as 1922 and 1923. Failing to cross this level was a sign of weakness and it should have been sold short. It went lower every year until December 1929, when it declined to a low of 6.

American Sugar Refining - 1921 low 48; September 1922, high 85; October 1924, declined to 36; September 1927, advanced to 95; February 1928, declined to 55; January 1929, advanced to 95, the same high as 1927. Failing to cross this level was a sign of weakness and it should have been sold short. November 1929, made low at 56, a support level, one point above the 1928 low; March 1930, rallied to 69.

Cuba Cane Sugar - Worked lower each year while other stocks were going up and finally in 1929 went into the receiver's hands.

Punta Alegre Sugar - This was one of the weak stocks in the sugar group from 1921 to 1930 and worked opposite to the trend of South Porto Rico Sugar. In April 1920, Punta made high at 120 and then started down. In June and October 1921, sold as low as 25; in January 1922, rallied to 53; then declined to 42 in November; in April 1923, advanced to 69; declined to 42 in July. Note this was the same low as made in November 1922, and a support level for a rally. In March 1924, it advanced to 67. Failing to cross the high of April 1923, indicated lower prices. In December 1924, it declined to 38; in January 1925, rallied to 47; and in July and October 1925, declined to 33, making a new low level and indicating a further decline. In February 1926, rallied to 47, making the same top as January 1925, and failing to cross it indicated lower prices. From April to July 1926, made a low of 33, the same low as it made in 1925. Holding this low level indicated support and a rally followed, reaching 49 in December 1926. Failing to get 3 points above the highs of 1925 and 1926 indicated that the main trend was down and the stock should have been sold short. In October 1927, it made a low of 27; in January and May 1928, rallied to 35, still showing down trend and a very feeble rally. In June 1929, declined to 15; then rallied to 22 in July. The main trend again turned down and it gradually worked lower until April 1930, when it declined to 3, the lowest in its history.

From this comparison you can see that you should have been playing the short side of Punta all along the same time when you were buying South Porto Rico and making money on both stocks in the same group which were running exactly opposite trends. Follow the rule - don't buy one stock in a group to follow another stock or sell one short to follow another unless the trend shows down.

South Porto Rico Sugar - This was the one exception in the sugar group that worked up while other sugar stocks were going down. This was plainly shown by the chart and indicated a strong position each year.

November 1921, low 26; March 1922, high 57; December 1922, low 33; March 1923, high 64, making a higher top and a higher bottom; August 1923, low 39, another higher bottom and a sign that the stock was going higher later; March 1924, high 95; October 1924, low 58. Around this level there was big accumulation during 1925, and in December 1925, it crossed 95, the high of 1924. A big advance followed. February 1926, high 147; March 1926, declined to 92, making bottom around the same levels where tops were reached in 1924 and 1925. This was a good support level. Then the trend turned up again and in May 1927, made final top at 197. Distribution took place and a stock dividend was declared. The new stock sold at 33 in February 1928; rallied in May and June to 49; then declined to 25 in December 1929. This was the one sugar stock that was making progressive tops and bottoms, that is, making higher tops and higher bottoms while other sugar stocks were making lower tops and lower bottoms. This proves my rule that one should buy the strongest stocks in the group and sell short the ones that are in the weakest position and show down trend. The man who bought other sugar stocks during the 1921 to 1929 Bull Campaign and expected them to follow South Porto Rico Sugar just because they were in the same group, lost big money and besides lost opportunities for making money in stocks in strong position.

TOBACCO STOCKS

In each group there is always a stock in strong position and one in the weakest position; therefore, it is well to have a chart on several stocks in each group. Look up some selling at high levels and some selling at low levels. As a rule, those selling at the highest levels are in the strongest position, while the ones selling at the lowest levels, in many cases, are in the weakest position and will go lower.

American Sumatra - Made high in 1918 at 135. The trend turned down and it went lower every year until May 1925, when it sold at 6. It went into the receiver' hands and a reorganization took place. The new stock started up from around 15 in April 1926; advanced to 69 in June 1927; declined to 46 in February 1928; and made a final high at 73 in August 1928. Then the trend turned down and in November 1929, it declined to 18, getting back within 3 points of the low of April 1926. This was a support level and a rally followed to 26 in February 1930; then declined to 16 in March 1930.

Reynolds Tobacco "B" - This was one of the strongest stocks in the tobacco group in 1921 and, in fact, during the whole campaign from 1921 to 1929. The charts plainly showed in 1920 and 1921 that this stock was being accumulated and was one of the best to buy in the group. December 1920, low 29½; January, 1921, low 31. It never sold lower and held in a narrow range during 1921, showing big accumulation and making slightly higher bottoms and higher tops. In the early part of 1922, the upswing started, subject to only minor reactions, until first top was reached in December 1927, when the high was 162. In April 1928, it declined to 128 where accumulation again took place. November 1928, final high 165, just 3 points above the high of 1927. Then a stock dividend was declared. The main trend continued down until November 1929, when it reached a low of 39. This last low was the same low made in January 1922, from which the big up move started, and was a support level where you should have bought with a stop at 36. The stock rallied to 58 in March 1930. From this, you can see how you could have made money buying this stock at very high levels after it had been going up for several years, because it still showed a strong position.

CHAPTER VIII
STOCKS OF THE FUTURE

When I wrote TRUTH OF THE STOCK TAPE, I said that the great fortunes in the future would be made in the airplane, chemical, and radio stocks. This prediction has been fulfilled, and these stocks have shown the greatest advances of any group.

Electric Stocks -This is the electrical age and electric stocks in the future will be among the good leaders. Electricity is being used in every business department, in manufacturing and in the home. New inventions are increasing yearly for electrical appliances. Electricity as a power is taking the place of steam with the railroad companies, and as improvements are made and electricity becomes cheaper, it will be used more and more. Therefore, companies manufacturing anything that uses electricity will prosper and their stocks should be watched.

Airplane Stocks -The airplane industry is in its infancy and will develop rapidly in the next few years. Fortunes can be made by selecting the right airplane stocks to buy at the right time.

Chemicals -Progress continues to be made in chemical stocks and new discoveries along this line will bring many chemical stocks into leadership and offer good opportunities for trading.

Radio and Wireless -The Radio stocks and those connected with wireless and television will prosper in the years to come and the good companies will increase earnings and their stocks will work higher.

Amusements -The talking picture industry is making rapid progress and the good companies will, no doubt, show big earnings in the future.

Natural Gas -Watch the oil companies that have natural gas and the companies which manufacture products from natural gas. There is a great future and big earnings for these companies.

But always remember that there are weak stocks in every group and strong ones. Therefore, in buying or selling, select the stock that shows the trend up or down and go with it.

AIRPLANE STOCKS

This group of stocks has already made fortunes for people who bought them at the right time and sold out at the right time, and many more great fortunes will be made by buying stocks in the airplane industry at the right time.

Curtiss-Wright -The two leading companies in the business were Wright and Curtiss. Curtiss made extreme low in August, 1921, when it sold at 1⅛. Then advanced to extreme high in May 1928, when it sold at 192½. Later it was consolidated with Wright Aeroplane Company. The Wright Brothers built the first airplane in the United States and made the first successful flight. Wright Aeroplane stock reached extreme low at 6 in January 1922, and sold at 299 in February 1929, an advance of 293 points in 7 years' time. The greater part of this advance was made in 1927 and 1928. The writer advised buying Wright Aeroplane stock all the way from $8 on up. After the consolidation of Curtiss and Wright, the new Curtiss-Wright stock made high in July and September 1929, at 30; in November 1929, sold at 6½, within ½ point of the low made by the old Wright stock in 1922. Curtiss-Wright rallied to 15 in April 1930. I consider this one of the best among the airplane companies, because it is composed of the two oldest companies in the business, which have made a success and will make success in the future. This is a good stock to buy on reactions.

United Aircraft & Transport -This company is controlled by the National City Bank and is already making money, earnings having been quite substantial in 1929. In March 1929, the stock sold at 67; then advanced to 162 in May 1929. It worked up too fast in its early stages and declined to a low of 31 in November 1929. In April 1930, advanced to 99. It will, no doubt, go much higher in later years. It is one of the good companies which I consider worth watching in the future and buying at the right time on reactions.

Fokker Aircraft -This Company is controlled by General Motors. It is well managed and will no-doubt show good earnings in the years to come. In December 1928, it sold as low as 17 and in May 1929, sold at 67. In October 1929, declined to 8 and in April 1930, rallied to 34. General Motors will, no doubt, be as successful in manufacturing airplanes as they have been in manufacturing and selling automobiles. This company will be one of the keen competitors of the other companies in the airplane industry, and the stock is good to buy on the reaction.

Bendix Aviation -This is another good airplane stock. It sold at 102 in August 1929; then declined to 25 in November and rallied to 57 in April 1930. It has future possibilities and should be watched and bought at the right time.

National Air & Transport -This is another good company and the stock should be watched for buying opportunities in the future. This stock will no doubt be merged with some of the other good companies.

Progress is rapid in the airplane industry because there is plenty of money behind it. New inventions and new discoveries are being made right along. The largest companies in the industry will acquire these new patents and make a success with them. There will be more consolidations and mergers in the airplane industry in the years to come. At present the best three are Curtiss-Wright, United Aircraft and Fokker. Keep up charts on the different airplane companies listed on the New York Curb and on the New York Stock Exchange; study them and you will be able to make money in this group of stocks.

STOCKS TO WATCH FOR FUTURE OPPORTUNITIES

There are always low-priced stocks which are being accumulated and getting in position for a big advance. You should keep charts on this class of stocks, because they possess opportunities for big profits when the moves get under way. Watch stocks that look as Bethlehem Steel, Crucible, General Motors, International Nickel, Jewel Tea, Montgomery Ward, Packard, U. S. Cast Iron Pipe and Wright Aeroplane did in 1915, 1917, 1920-1921, and 1923-1924. Buy them as soon as they break out of the trading area and show activity on increased volume.

The list of stocks given below is worth watching for future developments and you should keep up a yearly and monthly high and low chart on them, and as soon as they cross Resistance Levels and show up trend, buy them. Some of these stocks will make good and become active leaders.

American Agricultural Chemical, American Beet Sugar, American LaFrance, American Ship and Commerce, American Woolen, Austin Nichols, Aviation Corporation of Del., Booth Fisheries, Continental Motors, Consolidated Textile, Chicago, Milwaukee and St. Paul, Chicago Great Western, Dome Mines, Electric Boat, Fisk Rubber, Great Western Sugar, General Foods, Grigsby Grunow, Kelvinator, Kelly Springfield, Kresge Department Stores, Lee Rubber, Mullins Manufacturing, Mid-Continent Petroleum, Moon Motors, New York Air Brake, National Railways of Mexico, Panhandle Producers, Pure Oil, Reynolds Springs, Standard Brands, Standard Oil of New York, Superior Oil, Transcontinental Oil, Texas Pacific Coal and Oil, U. S. Rubber, Ward Baking, Wilson & Co.

FUTURE OF U. S. RUBBER

The United States Rubber Company is one of the largest manufacturing companies in this line. In the early part of 1929 the du Ponts acquired a large interest in this company. The stock declined to 15 in the 1929 panic, the lowest since 1907. I believe that this stock has great future possibilities, from the way it acts on the chart. I am sure that the du Pont interests believe that it has possibilities, the same as General Motors had in 1921, or they would not have put their money into it. You should keep up a chart on U. S. Rubber and watch it. As soon as it shows that the main trend has turned up, buy it and then follow it up and pyramid as long as it shows up trend.

Men like J. P. Morgan and the du Ponts do not buy a stock to sell in a short time. They buy it to hold for the long pull and because the company possesses possibilities of paying larger dividends. At the price at which U. S. Rubber is selling at this writing, March 1930, it is probably one of the very best stocks on the list selling at this level. This does not mean that it may not go lower, but it does mean that the chances for profits are much greater in the future than any other stock you could buy around the same price.

Your object should always be to buy the stock that has the greatest possibilities but remember that you must limit your risk with a stop loss order. Something unexpected might happen and U. S. Rubber might go very much lower; therefore, if the trend turns down, you had better be out of it.

VANADIUM STEEL

This company has practically a monopoly on Vanadium and is engaged in the chemical industry. Its earnings have been good for many years. Recently the company acquired valuable property in Virginia, which will enhance its earnings in future years. The volume of stock outstanding and the floating supply is very small, which makes it easy for pools to put it up. Since it sold at 37½ in November 1929, it has advanced to the highest level in its history, 142⅜, on April 23, 1930, up 105 points in a little over 5 months' time, advancing over twice as much as U. S. Steel. Recently it has been rumored that there is virtually a corner in the stock. This will be a good stock to trade in for several years to come and will probably sell at very high levels. It is good to buy on reactions when the charts show that the trend is up. You should be careful about going short of it on account of the small floating supply of stock. If you do go short, protect it with a close stop loss order.

CHAPTER IX
FUTURE FACTS AND DEVELOPMENTS

STOCKS OVERBOUGHT

It requires a long period of time to establish public confidence in any group of stocks, but once a stock or a group of stocks becomes a public favorite, it is overbought. Traders get too optimistic and overconfident, overtrade and buy too much and the insiders, of course, have an opportunity to sell out stocks which they have held for a long period of time.

The railroad stocks were in this position before the Civil War and worked lower until 1893 to 1896, when most of them went into the hands of a receiver. Then came the Reconstruction Period and the McKinley boom. Railroad stocks came into favor again and had big advances, reaching top in 1906; then followed the 1907 panic, and the rails had a severe decline. Again, in 1909, the railroad stocks advanced but did not get back to their previous high levels. The public overbought at the top and on the way down. The rails started to decline and continued to go lower until 1917 and 1921 when final bottoms were reached.

This same condition now prevails in the automobile stocks. The public learned about automobile stocks in 1915 and 1916, when they had their big advances and again in 1919, but from 1924 to 1929 the public bought automobile stocks on a scale greater than ever before in any group of stocks. Therefore, the motors are greatly overbought and most of the companies are greatly overcapitalized. They have paid stock dividends and increased their stock to such an extent that they cannot pay dividends during the years of depression to come. Therefore, the automobile stocks will be among the best short sales in the coming bear market.

The same condition prevails in the public utilities. These stocks have had such rapid advances and their earnings have increased so enormously during the past few years that speculators and investors have bought on a large scale from 1924 to 1929. Public utility companies will be subject to adverse legislation and Government investigation during the next few years. These stocks are too high in most cases and even if nothing unfavorable happens in the way of Government action, they will decline anyway, because they are in weak hands, and with the public in and the insiders out, there will be a long trend down.

PRODUCTION AND CONSUMPTION

It is very important to watch production in any manufacturing line as the tendency is always towards overproduction, especially in boom times and in the last stages of a bull market or in the last stage of a wave of prosperity. Business men always get too optimistic at the end of a wave of prosperity and expect larger consumption than later materializes and of course, when production is greater than consumption, prices decline. Just the same after a long bear market or a long wave of depression, business people become pessimistic and under-estimate the public requirements or consumption. This causes prices to rise because production has fallen below consumption. Competition always gets keener near the top when more is being produced that can be sold, and the result is a decline in prices whether it be commodities or manufactured articles. The stock market discounts these changes in advance.

INVESTMENT TRUSTS

Investment Trusts in this country came into prominence during the last stage of the 1921 to 1929 Bull Campaign. It has been estimated that between January 1 and September 1, 1929, the public put between 4 and.5 billion dollars into investment trusts. The last final grand rush in the stock market, which occurred during the months of July and August, was caused to a great extent by buying by investment trusts. These new trusts found it: so easy to get money from the public that they rushed into the market and bought stocks regardless of price and without considering that they were buying at the top of a bull market which had been running for over 8 years. This together with short covering and public buying, carried stocks to unreasonable heights and to levels where there were no dividend prospects and earnings which warranted the stocks selling at these levels. Of course, the investment trusts did not foresee the coming panic and held on and hoped, with the result that many of them found their original capital cut in half or more.

There are some good investment trusts, but there are many which are nothing more than discretionary pools, operating in the market without any scientific basis, therefore their success cannot be any greater than that of the ordinary trader, who buys and sells without any definite plan. If stocks went up all of the time, then investment trusts could make money because they buy and do not sell short, but when we have a bear market lasting for several years, investment trusts will not only fail to earn any dividend on the money, but a large portion of the capital invested will be wiped out. Therefore, the public who put money in the investment trusts will fare no better than if they had bought stocks at the tops themselves. In the Summer of 1929 the buying by investment trusts helped many pools to unload stocks that they never would have been able to sell at such high prices otherwise. During the coming years there will no doubt be many failures among investment trusts. Their stocks will decline and the public will become disgusted and sell out the stocks of the investment trusts. This will force the investment trusts to liquidate the stocks which they have bought at inflated values.

The investor or trader who buys investment trusts should certainly look before he leaps and investigate before he buys, as the ones that will be successful are few and far between, especially when there is liable to be an irregular bear market for several years to come. When the day comes that investment trusts start to liquidate stocks, and investors get scared and start to sell, then we will have the investors' panic.

MERGERS AND COMBINATIONS

The present period of mergers and combinations, which began in 1924, is the greatest in the history of the world. To get the significance of it and what the final result of this gigantic increase in stocks will be, we must go back to 1899 to 1902, when the United States Steel Corporation was formed, with its so-called 5 million shares of watered common stock. The American Smelting Trust and Amalgamated Copper were formed about the same time and other consolidations. The public was loaded up with watered stocks which could not pay dividends. A decline followed in 1903-1904; then there was another wild wave of speculation which culminated in 1906. In 1907, the real panic came and the gains of 3 to 5 years were wiped out in a few months. What was the cause of this severe decline? The public was loaded up with stocks which were inflated and could not pay dividends on the increased capitalization; the banks were loaded with loans, and a money panic followed.

When we consider the consolidations and mergers which have taken place during the past few years and the enormous increase in the capital stock, it is easy to figure how impossible it is for these companies to continue to earn their dividends during a period of even two years' poor business, and suppose we should have a period of 5 to 7 years of depression, what would happen? Stocks are of no value to anyone unless they earn money, and they are only worth what you can sell them for when you want to sell them. The fact that a stock sold at 400 in 1929 will not help the investor when it is selling at 200 in 1931, because his capital has shrunk 50 per cent and he can only get for the stock what someone will pay for it. People are hoping for the impossible. They expect a company to earn as much dividends on 10 or 20 million shares of stock as it has earned on 5 to 10 million, which is impossible over a long period of time. Therefore, the inevitable must be a long period of liquidation, followed by a final crash or panic, which will ruin hundreds of thousands of investors who hold on and hope until it is too late.

The wise man will get out and wait. It is better to be safe than sorry; better to keep pour money without getting any interest or dividends than to risk it on an investment that will wipe out 50 per cent or more of your capital. The greatest damage comes from too much hope and optimism. There is no question but what the optimist is the greatest menace to prosperity. The pessimist is the balance wheel, and we need him to sound the note of warning. It has been said : "The difference between the pessimist and optimist is droll; one sees the dough nut and the other sees the hole." Now is the time when we need a man who can see the hole that is going to be made in the investors' pocket-books, if they continue to look at the dough nut and shut their eyes to the painful fact that the hole is there. The hole is what you fall into. Watch for the hole! It is always there.

REPARATION BONDS

Liquidation in the stock market during the Fall of 1929 prepared the money market for the reception of large bond issues. At this writing call money is loaning around 2 per cent. Bankers and bond brokers are looking forward to the time when the European reparation bonds will be sold in this country. While the writer does not advise buying them, nevertheless, hundreds of thousands of people will buy them if they are offered here. This will tie up a lot of money that will later be termed "frozen loans." Should trouble start in Europe again or war break out, these bonds will decline and may be repudiated. Always remember in Wall Street and in the financial game that anything can happen, therefore be prepared for the unexpected. The American public has billions of dollars already invested in the European countries and if the time ever comes, which is probable, that investors face the loss of all this money, or at least a part of it, and they try to sell their bonds, this will help to bring about panic and depression and hurt all kinds of business. If a large amount of the reparation bonds are sold in this country and the money is taken away to foreign countries, it will naturally effect our money market later and cause higher rates for money.

INVESTORS' PANIC

About every 20 years there is an investors' panic or a severe depression, brought about by investors selling stocks at low levels. This is due to a prolonged decline and loss of confidence. Buying power having been reduced and investment selling continually coming into the market, force prices lower and lower until banks call loans on high-class investment stocks, with the final result of a wide-open break or a sharp, severe decline. This occurred in 1837 to 1839, 1857, 1873, 1893, 1896, 1914 and 1920 to 1921. The panic of 1929 was not an investors' panic. It was a gamblers' panic.

Various causes have produced these different panics, but the real basis behind all of them has been the money market. The banks, having become overloaded with loans during periods of prosperity, forced selling and produced the panic. Most bankers get too optimistic after a prolonged period of prosperity; then after a prolonged decline and business depression they become too pessimistic and are afraid to make loans. In fact, instead of making new loans they call old loans, which makes the situation worse than it would be otherwise. It is the same with most of the newspapers. They know that it is popular to talk optimistic and they go to the extreme in good times and then when conditions get bad, they generally paint the picture blacker than it really is.

Certainly, during all of these panics, some of the brokers and banks must have seen the handwriting on the wall and have known just exactly what was coming, but they never told their customers about it. Then the investor must stop, look and listen. He must think for himself and not depend upon his banker or his broker to get him out of the market at the right time, because past history proves that their advice at critical times cannot be depended upon.

The coming investors' panic will be the greatest in history, because there are at least 15 to 25 million investors in the United States who hold stocks in the leading corporations, and when once they get scared, which they will after years of decline, then the selling will be so terrific that no buying power can withstand it. Stocks are so well distributed in the hands of the public that since the 1929 panic many people think that the market is panic-proof, but this seeming strength is really the weakest feature of the market. The public has never been good leaders and never will be, because their hopes and fears are easily excited. If stocks were all in the hands of a few strong men, then investors and the country would be safe, but when they are in the hands of millions of people who are unorganized and without leadership, then the situation is dangerous. A wise man will sell before it is too late. The public will hold on and hope; then all will become scared at the same time and sell when nobody wants to buy, thus precipitating a panic. This was what caused the 1929 panic. The speculators and gamblers all got scared and sold at the same time.

Greed and love of money will cause the next panic and the love of money will be the cause of the next war. "War is hell!" You might ask what that has to do with stocks. War has always caused panics. War is coming and a panic is coming in stocks, and this time the panic in stocks may be the cause of war. People often get a misconception of an idea or quote things wrong. We often hear people say "Money is the root of all evil." They think they are quoting the Bible, but they are not. The Bible says, "The love of money is the root of all evil." In fact, the love of money and the quest for power has been the cause of all wars, as history proves. Love of money has been the cause of all financial troubles and depressions in the past, and the coming panic will be the greatest the world has ever known, because there is more money in the United States than ever before, therefore more to fight for. Men fight harder for money than anything else, once they see it slipping away.

AFTERWORD

I have written this book at the earnest solicitation of thousands of people who bought TRUTH OF THE STOCK TAPE and have kindly said that it was the best ever written on the stock market. It gives me great pleasure to have helped others to make a greater success in the hazardous game of Wall Street. If TRUTH OF THE STOCK TAPE* was the best book, I have tried and hope I have succeeded in making the WALL STREET STOCK SELECTOR a better book. I have written what I know from experience others need. I have discovered the rules and methods through making mistakes and losses myself. I have been through the Wall Street mill for nearly 30 years and time has proven to me what a man needs to make a success in speculation. I am confident that those who follow my rules will never regret it and I shall feel well repaid for helping the other fellow who is trying to help himself.

---

* More books of W.D.Gann at www.therichestmaninbabylon.org
Books for the self-investor

Printed in the United States
147767LV00004B/6/P